This Breathing House

∞

Bharti Kher

Hauser & Wirth Publishers

Freud Museum London

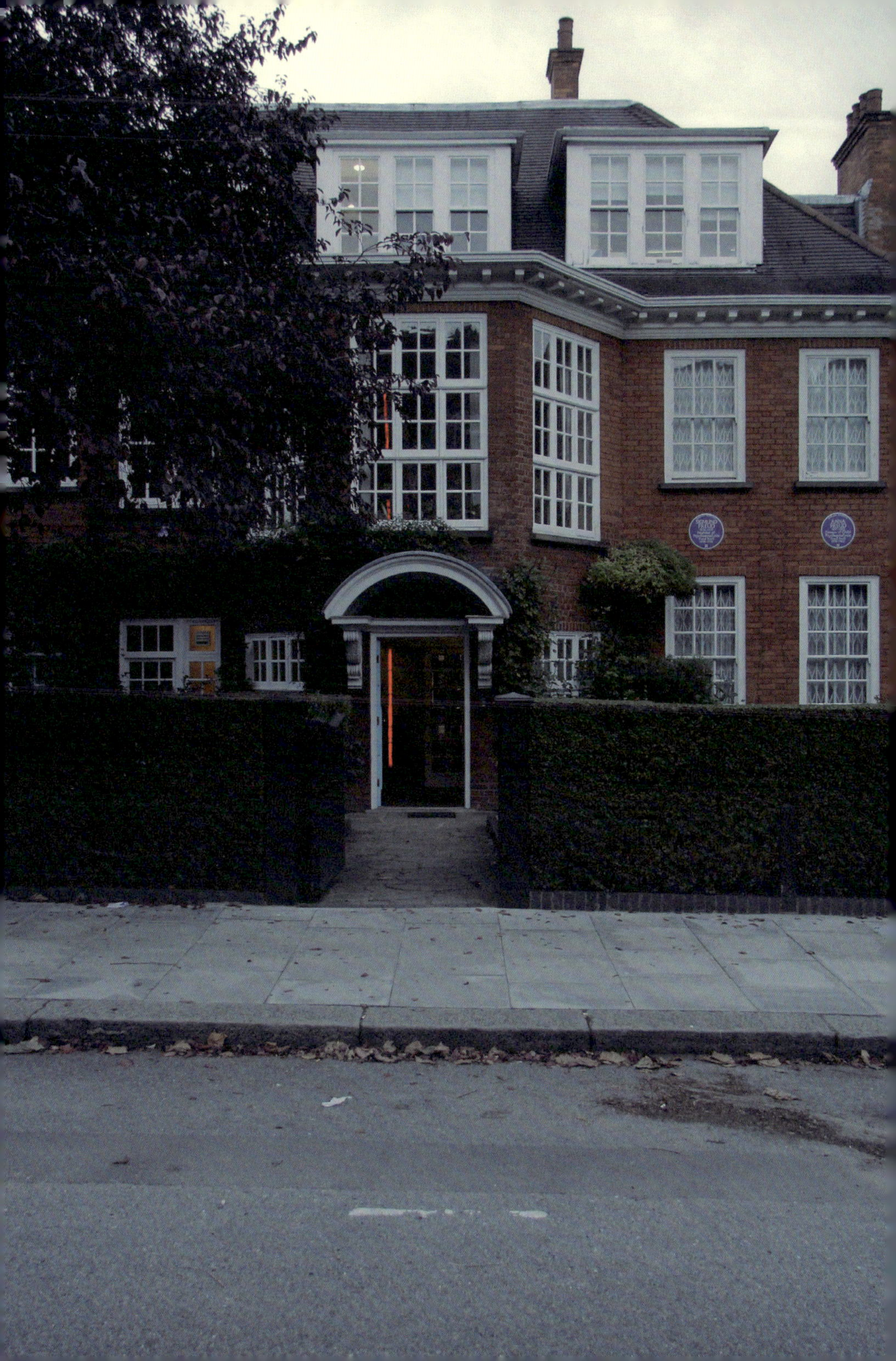

Foreword

The Freud Museum London at 20 Maresfield Gardens was the final home of Sigmund Freud, the founder of psychoanalysis, and his daughter Anna, pioneer of child analysis. It was here that the Freud family settled in 1938 after fleeing Nazi persecution in Austria.

Unusually for a refugee from the Nazis, Sigmund Freud was able to bring his possessions, including his collection of around two thousand antiquities, out of Vienna where he had lived and worked for most of his life. Transported to London, these possessions were reassembled in Freud's new home, a substantial house in a leafy suburb. Here the elderly Freud was again working in a unique environment of his own making, surrounded by his books, his antiquities, and the original psychoanalytic couch.

20 Maresfield Gardens opened as a museum in 1986, and has become both a popular London historic house museum and a renowned international centre for research, education and innovative public programmes. The Museum's aim is to preserve the legacy of Sigmund and Anna Freud, and to be a centre for learning and discussion on psychoanalysis today.

Over the last twenty years The Freud Museum has also developed an impressive reputation for its imaginative, innovative programme of exhibitions by renowned contemporary artists.

The Freud Museum provides not a white cube gallery, but a unique space, a potent mix of family home, laboratory of ideas, doctor's office, and lastly a museum. As if in a time capsule, here are the iconic couch, scene of so many recounted dreams and memories, the cherished collection of classical antiquities, Freud's desk and extensive library. For many years the house was home to Sigmund's youngest child Anna, analyst to countless children, and her life and work too are part of this space.

Artists engage with the writings of Sigmund or Anna Freud and the unique collections of the Museum to produce exhibitions closely aligned to the subject matter of the Museum. Displaying art in the Museum has proved a successful way of engaging the public with psychoanalytic ideas, and bringing in new audiences.

Bharti Kher was born and educated in Britain, and moved to India after graduating from university. She has built an enviable reputation for producing art which straddles complex subjects and cultural differences combined with dark humour and infectious charm. Her richly varied work, encompassing painting, sculpture, everyday objects and installation is endlessly imaginative, richly colourful and appealing.

In *This Breathing House*, Bharti Kher's inquiry into the realm of the domestic and its protagonists finds its perfect counterpart in the Freud Museum London. Bharti Kher's exhibition is a dialogue with the house, exploring Freud's family life as well as his theories. Vivid and full of history, the artist calls into being the voices that echo through the house and refers to Maresfield Gardens as an organism, a "breathing entity".

Bharti Kher overlays, subverts, conserves and erases memories – of herself and of her own life, of her family and of the people who lived here. The mythological creatures Bharti uses in her work resonate too with Sigmund Freud's own myriad collection of extraordinary objects.

Bharti Kher's art demands a second look, a closer investigation, to get under its skin – an important component of much of her work – and reveal a deeper meaning. In this the artist's works displayed in *This Breathing House* echo the explorations and revelations of psychoanalysis, the words, dreams, memories and fleeting images which are so bound up with the history of Sigmund and Anna Freud's home in Maresfield Gardens.

— Carol Seigel, Director, Freud Museum London

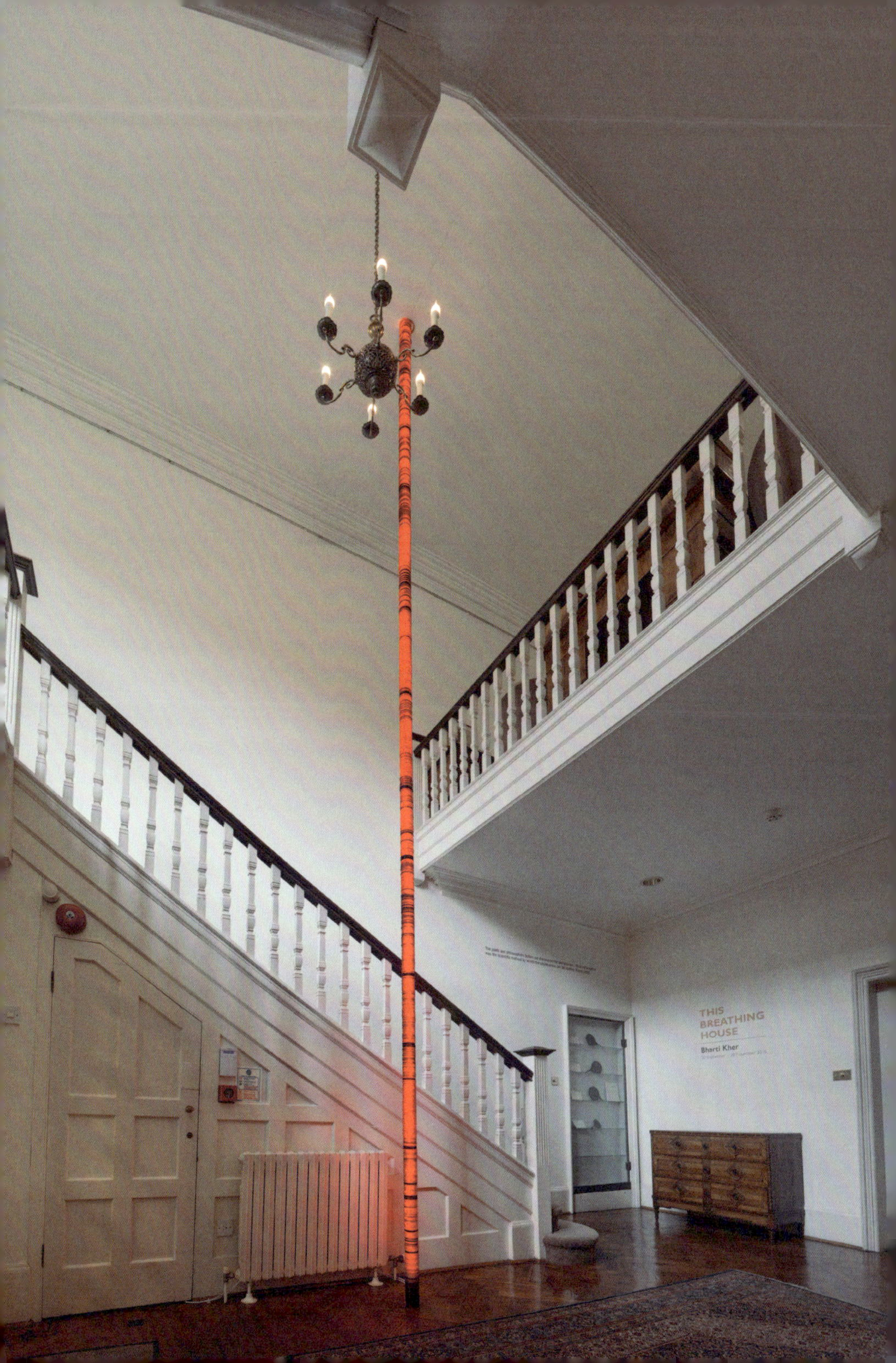

THIS
BREATHING
HOUSE
Bharti Kher

A
Rhizomatic
Invasion

∞

Stephanie
Rosenthal

1.

Rhizomes

This Breathing House is one exhibition amongst many and yet very special. It is on show in the Freud Museum and in a sense it could be equated to the Freud Museum; at the same time it also reveals the interconnective, subterranean root system of Bharti Kher's works.

> "Before long I learned that you had spent a lifetime equally devoted to the conviction that words are not good enough. Not only not good enough, but corrosive to all that is good … Once we name something, you said, we can never see it the same way again. All that is unnameable falls away, gets lost, is murdered. You called this the cookie-cutter function of our minds."[1]
>
> — Maggie Nelson

Kher's works originate in her studio and it is as though they are connected by an umbilical cord to their place of origin, only to acquire another dimension as site-specific works by virtue of the way that Kher installs them.[2]

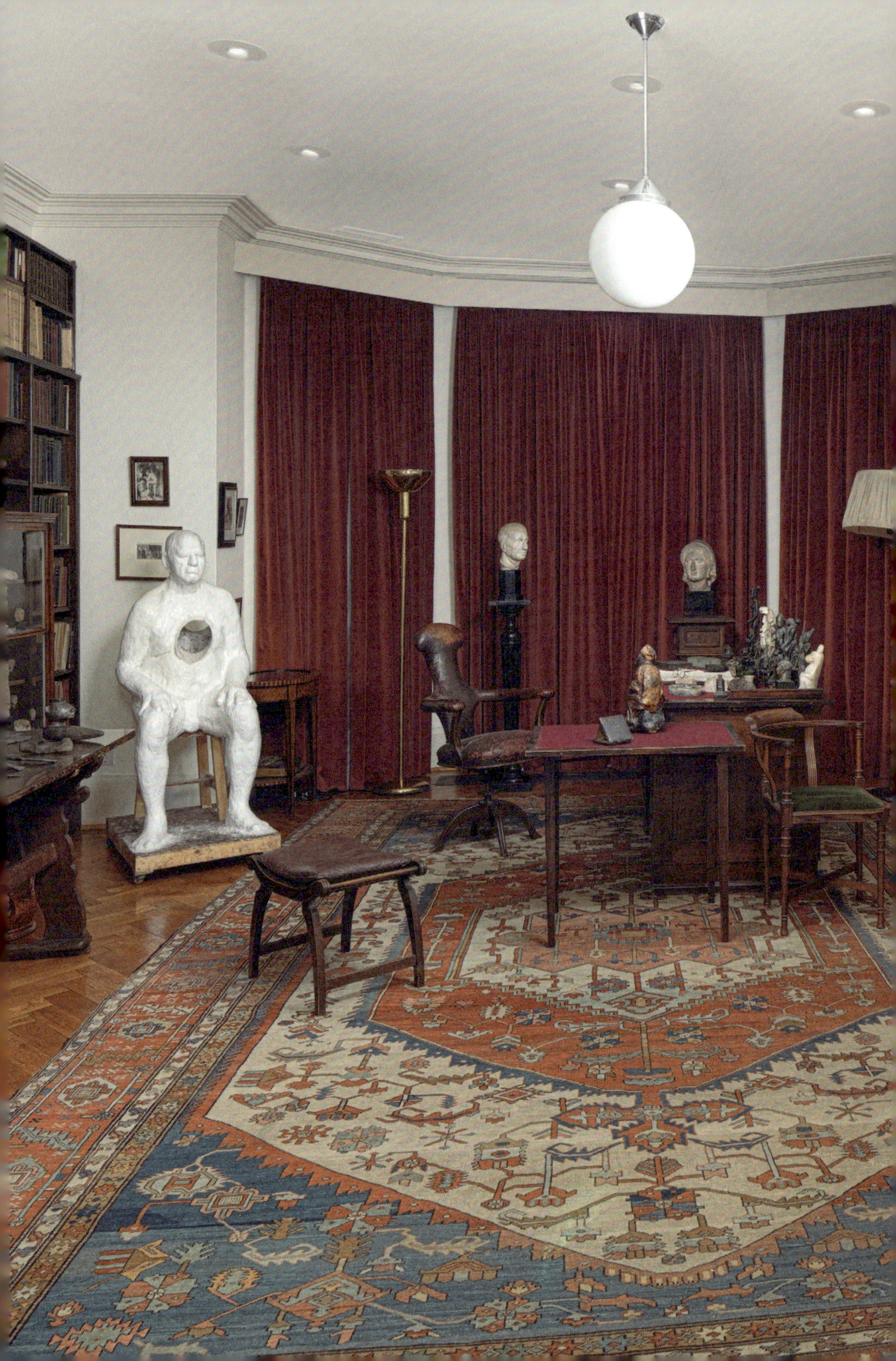

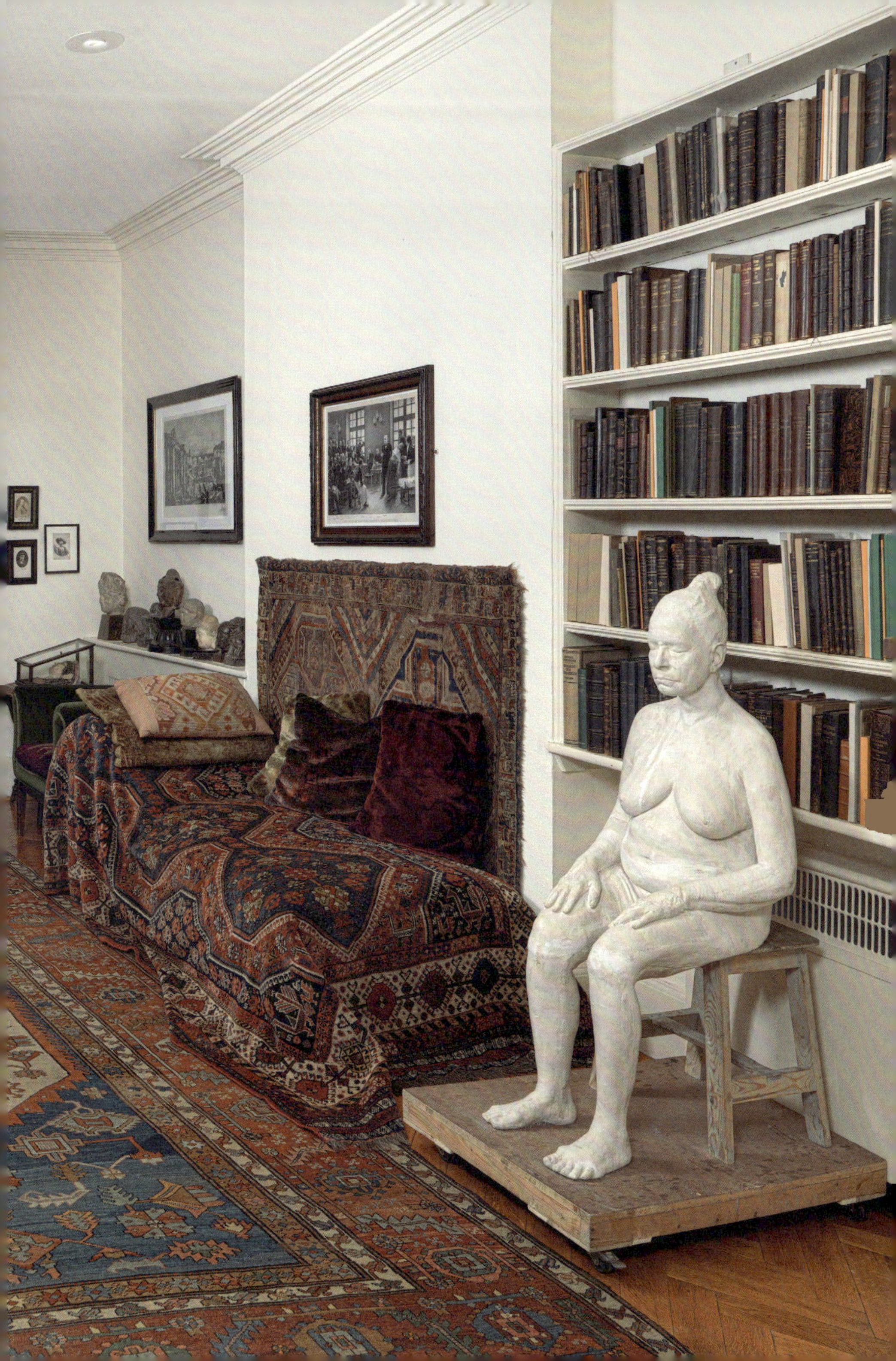

2.

The House

"Houses often have a symbolic meaning in dreams and generally relate to the dreamer's state of mind. Freud interpreted the occurrence of a house in a dream as a reflection of the female. In psychological dream-interpretation the house is often associated with feminine intuition and powers of observation. Freud also regarded dream images of houses as having a sexual aspect, which has become something of an exception in the modern interpretation of dreams."[3]

Freud's house demanded to become part of the installation. It is a two-storey building with a cellar, an attic and a garden. It is impossible to prevent one's thoughts from turning to its occupants and their complicated relationships. Martha and Sigmund Freud moved into this house in 1938 with their youngest daughter, Anna. The latter's lifelong companion, Dorothy Burlingham, joined them there later. Although Anna Freud carried out secretarial work for her father, today she is above all known for her own psychotherapeutic work with children. Her methods are still taught today and there are various Anna Freud Centres and Institutes around the world.

Kher superimposes, subverts, conserves, eradicates and layers memories – of her own and in their own right, memories of her own family and of the people who lived in this house.

Kher's works literally occupy the house and transform the building into a pulsating organism, a body. Casts of her parents, *Mother* and *Father*, in Freud's study open up an additional, imaginary space. *Bloodline* (made from glass bangles) runs through the building like a spinal cord and *Equilibrium* marks the core of the building. Wax sculptures occupy the original dining room, while collages on double-sided pages from children's books are found on the floor where Anna Freud lived. *Take something for something* is on display in Anna's room. Other sculptural works are distributed throughout the house.

Below ground there is a complex system of interconnections, rhizomes, a profusion of roots. They connect by means of mental leaps, horizontal juxtapositions, with no need for hierarchical interpretation. The visitor – entering from outside – becomes part of this exhibition-rhizome, encountering installations and potentially connecting with them, being affected by them.

Mother, 2016
Plaster of Paris, wood
140 × 63 × 96 cm

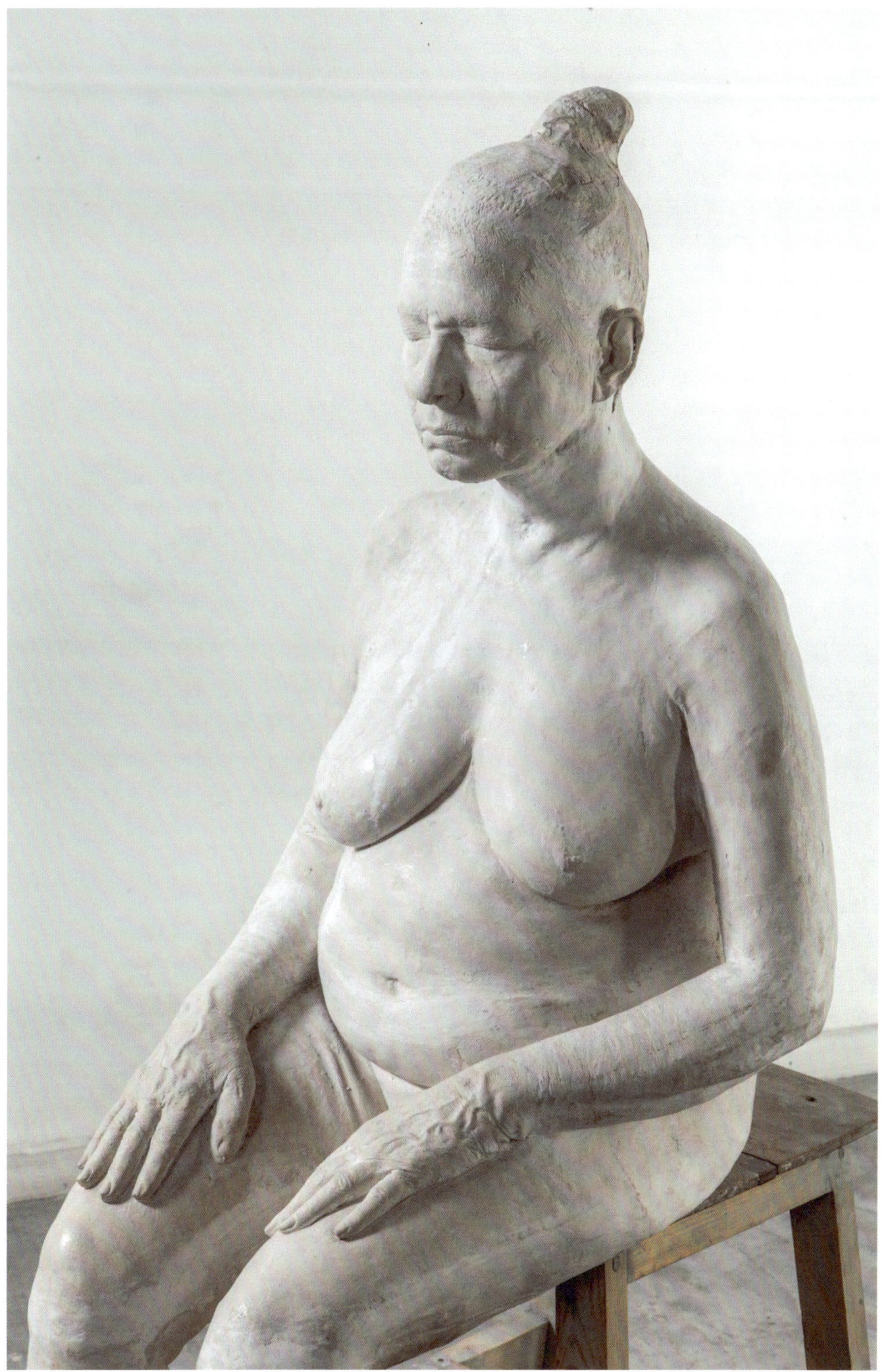

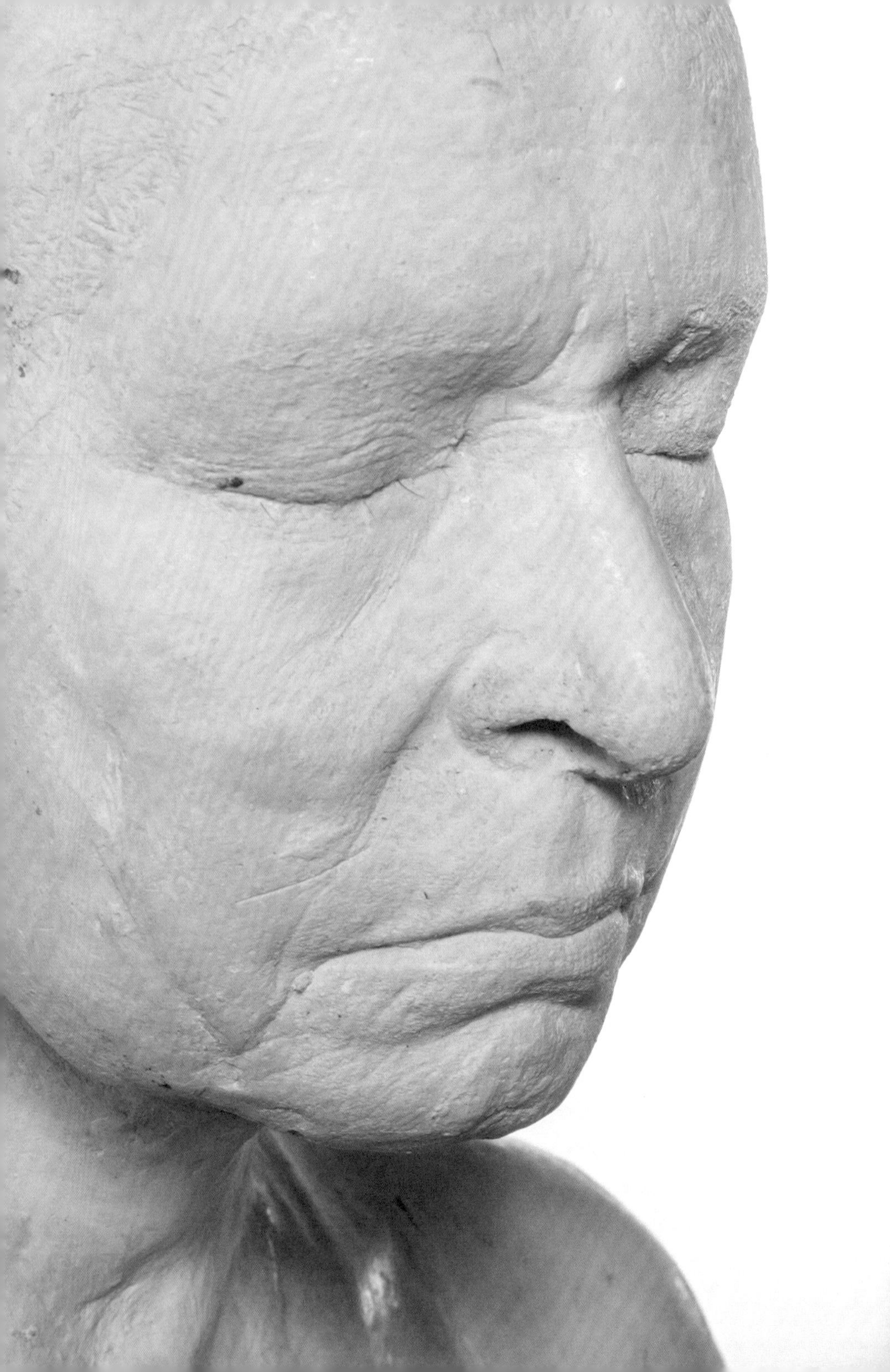

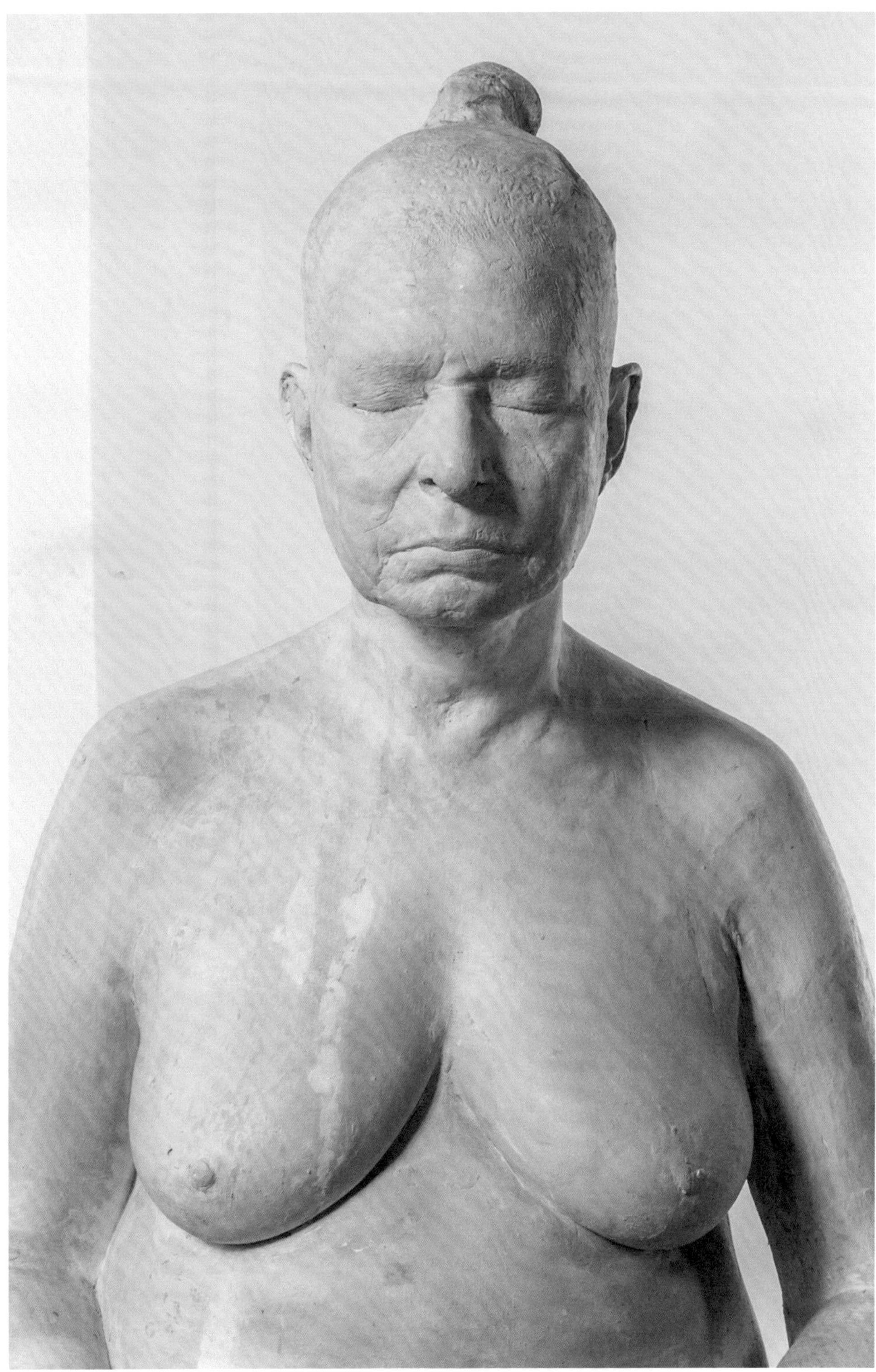

3.

Body Cast / Imprint

"Making an imprint [*empreinte*]: producing a mark
by means of the pressure of a body on a surface . . .
A frequent connotation of the word 'imprint' – unlike
'trace', perhaps, although that needs to be discussed
in greater detail – is that the result endures, that the
action gives rise to a 'permanent mark'. Be that as
it may, an imprint presumes a support or substrate,
an *action* that creates it (generally involving pressure,
or at least contact), and a mechanical result, that is
to say, a *mark*, either sunken or standing proud."[5]

— Georges Didi-Huberman

In the two plaster casts Kher's parents' bodies are seen naked, with
no paraphernalia of any kind. They appear vulnerable, quiet, inward.
Kher ascribes no meaning to them, but lets them speak for themselves.
Every little detail of their bodies and their skin was imprinted into the
plaster before being turned inside-out. All their distinguishing features
are inscribed into the plaster, archived there.

"When or how do new kinship systems mime older
nuclear-family arrangements and when or how do
they radically re-contextualize them in a way that
constitutes a rethinking of kinship? How can you tell;
or, rather, who's to tell? Tell your girlfriend to find a
different kid to play house with, your ex would say,
after we first moved in."[6]

— Maggie Nelson

They are sitting on stools, their feet on the floor, hands on their thighs, eyes closed. There is a hint of tension in the mother's face. It is concentrated but calm – as though passing time were of no matter. Her hair is firmly tied back for the casting.

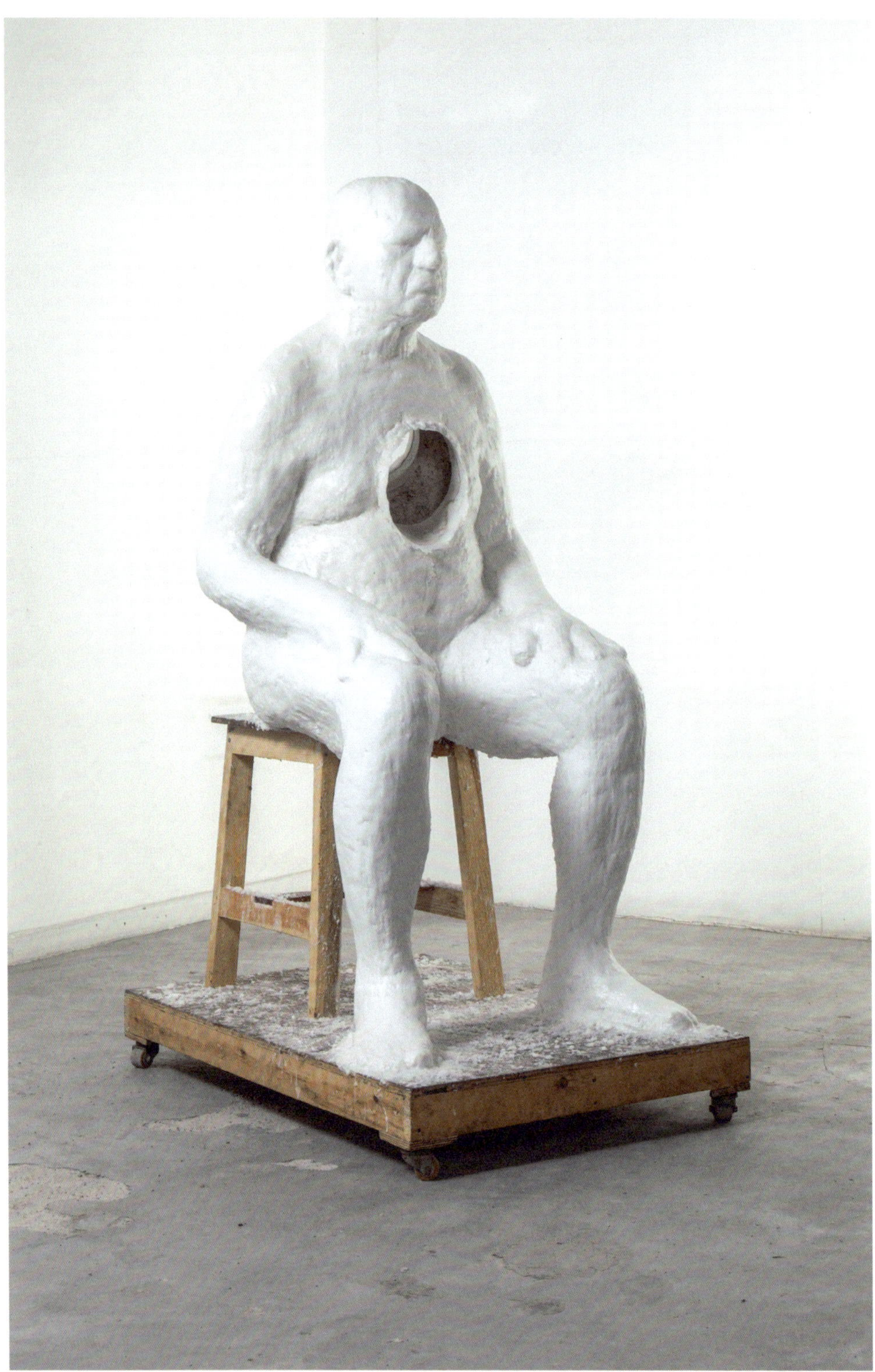

Father, 2016
Plaster of Paris, wood, wax
148 × 70 × 94 cm

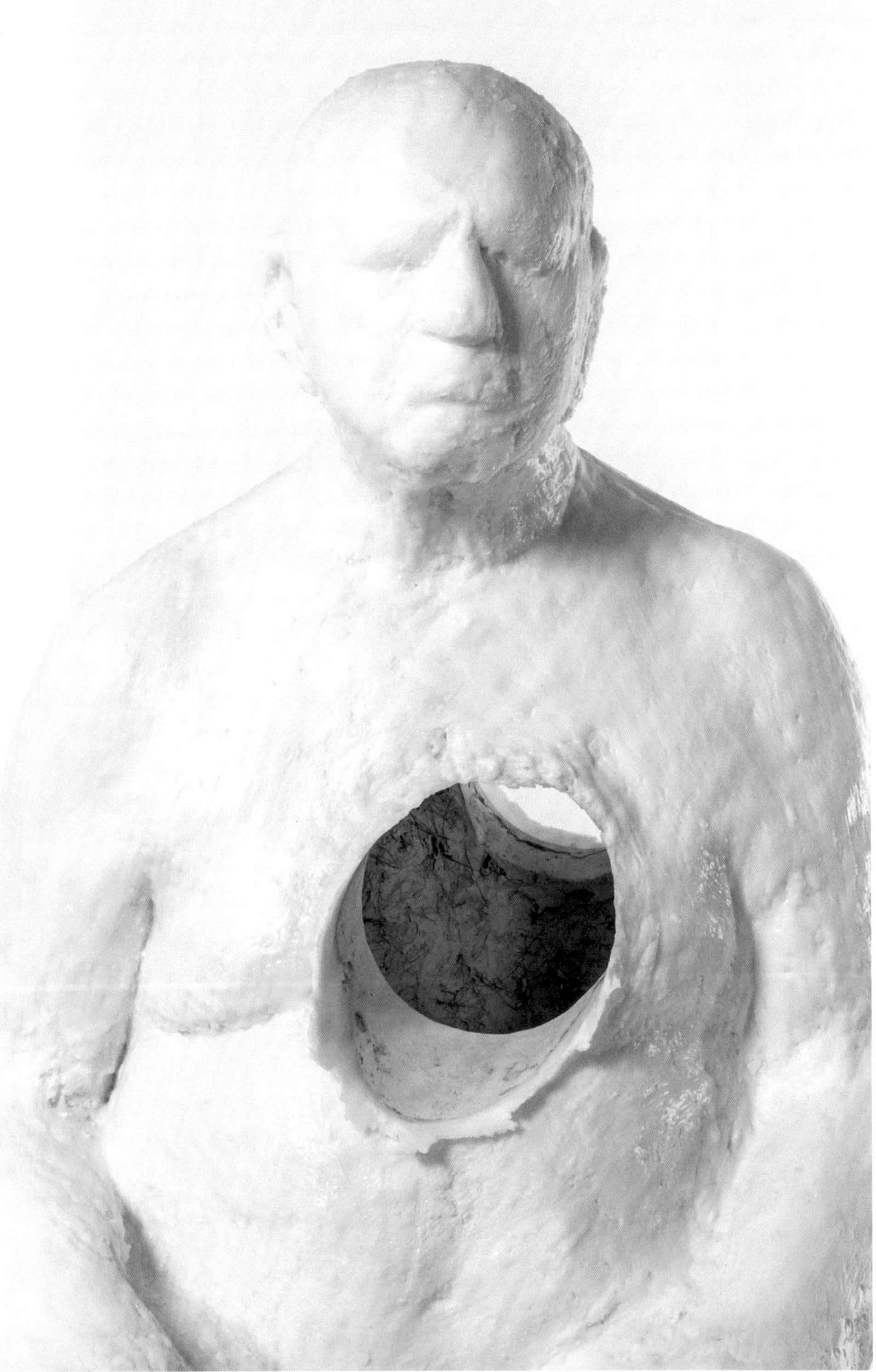

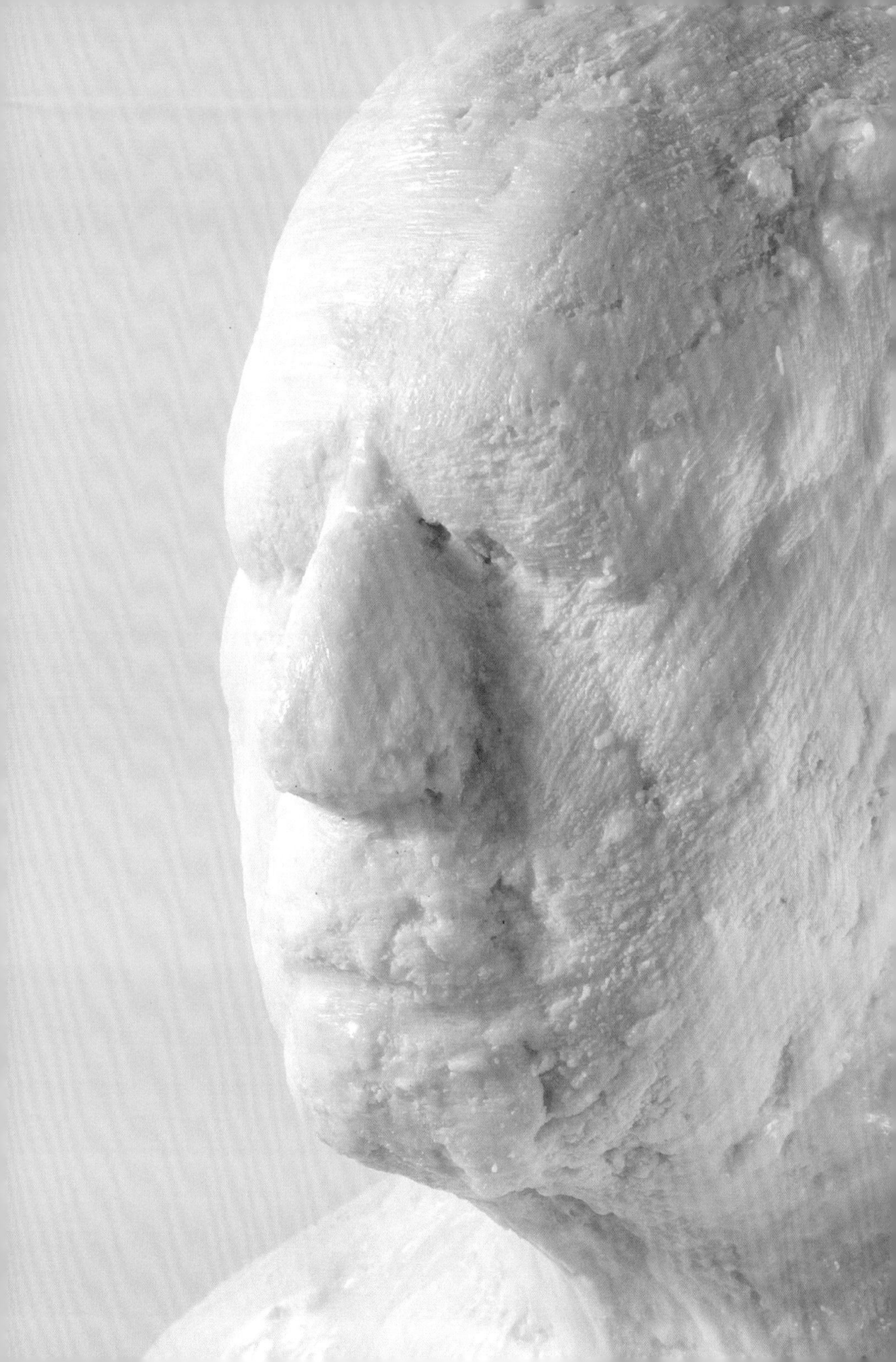

4.

Parents

"Is there something inherently queer about pregnancy
itself, insofar as it profoundly alters one's 'normal' state,
and occasions a radical intimacy with – and radical
alienation from – one's body? How can an experience
so profoundly strange and wild and transformative also
symbolise or enact the ultimate conformity? Or is this just
another disqualification of anything tied too closely to the
female animal from the privileged term *(in this case, non-
conformity, or radicality)? What about the fact that Harry
is neither male nor female? I am special – a two for one,
his character Valentine explains in By Hook or By Crook.*"[7]

— Maggie Nelson

Between 2012 and 2014 Kher created a series of plaster casts of
sex workers in Kolkata, also naked, each on a stool, again presenting
nothing but their bodies. Kher is now continuing this exploration
of the human body with her parents as subjects. "It's a strange and
cathartic process casting. When you caress the skin and rub the plaster
gently over and over so that all the pores and creases are etched and
filled with plaster, it's like encasing and mummifying a living being.
You are trying to capture their breath, to find the imprint of their minds
and thoughts and the secrets of the soul. Give me your essence and be
light for that time. What the cast carries only the model can give."[8]

She thus discovers, investigates and questions her parents' bodies, which bear on them the marks of the passage of time, as she attempts to focus on her relationship with them, to see it anew, to revisit the familiar. "You see them so much, you can't always read them. Familiarity makes you not see some things."[9]

"There is, emphatically, a radical difference between a form created from an impression and all kinds of *imitation* in the classical sense: imitation presumes distance, visuality and mediation."[10]

— Georges Didi-Huberman

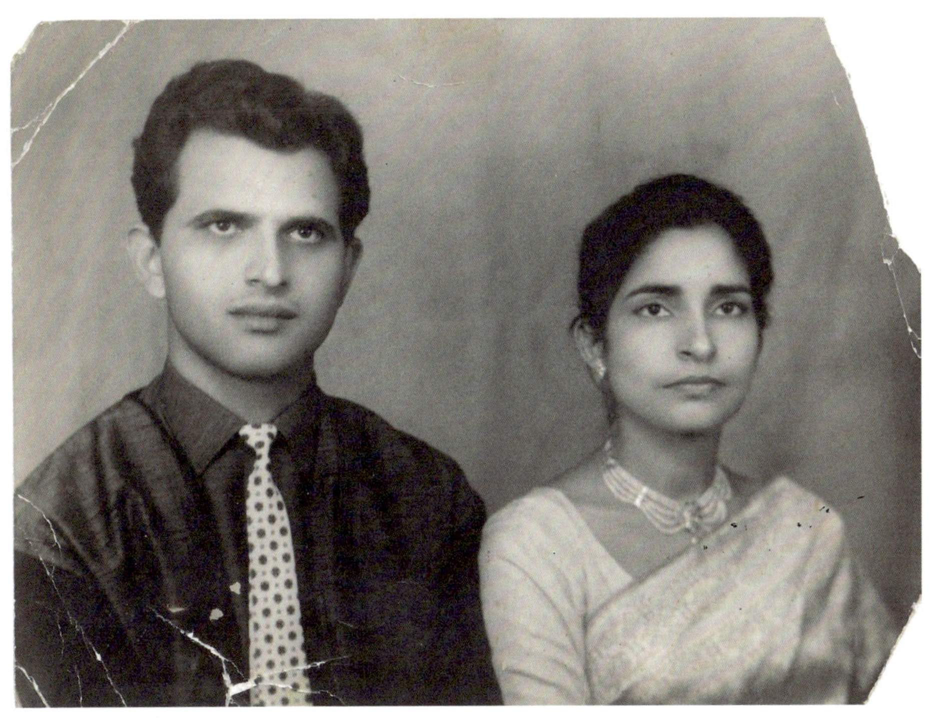

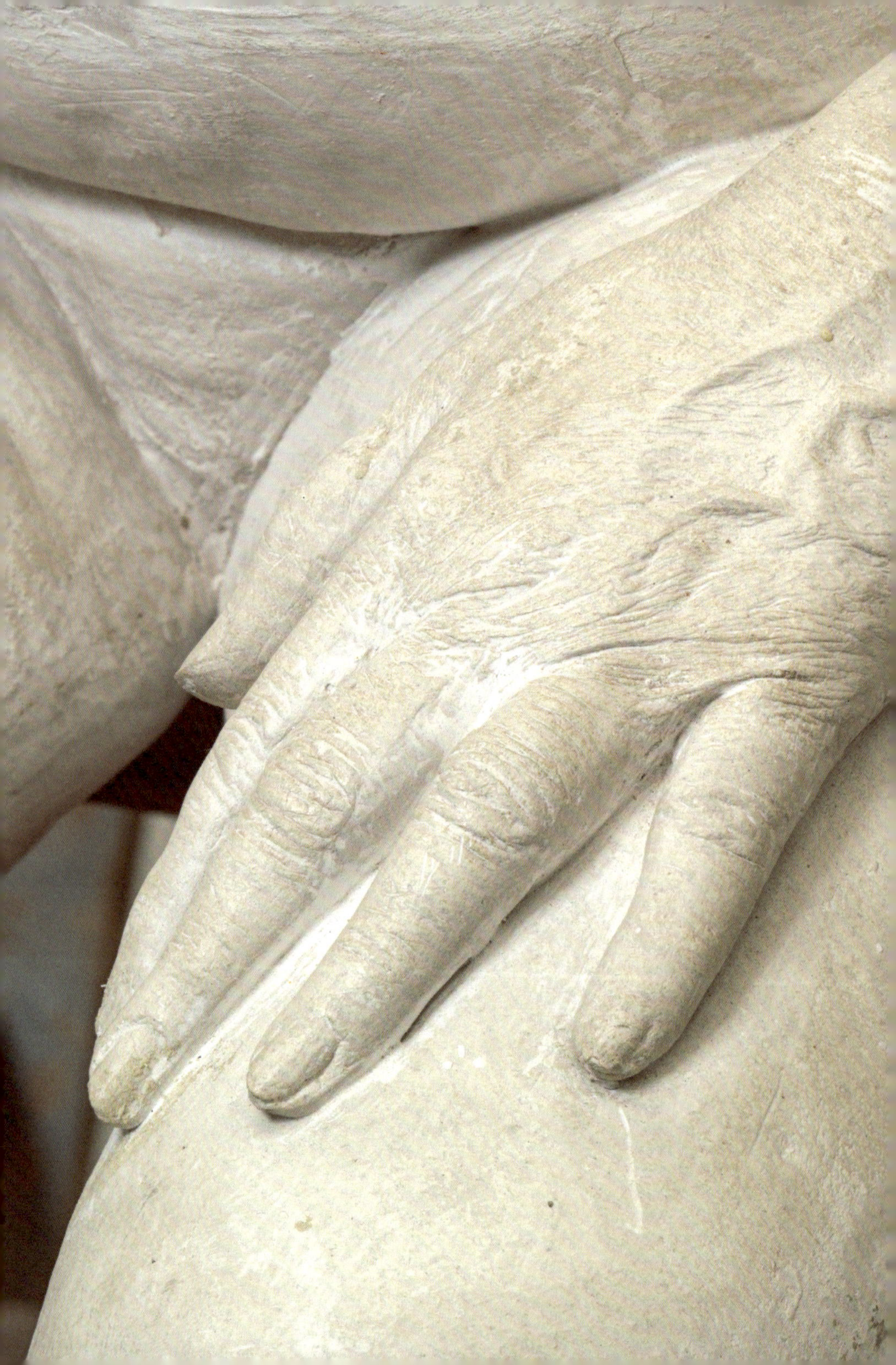

5.

Skin

Skin is the primary carrier of memory. These sculptures deal with "what was perhaps suggested through the casting of the skin through the memory of this tactility of plaster and how it impregnates the skin and somehow takes the essence through the pores. . . . It's almost as if you look away from somebody to understand, to hear them, to see them. . . . You have to not just use the eyes to see, you have to also remember and also somehow bring together your experience and forgive."[11]

6.

Preserving / Wax

Kher finishes the figure of her father with an additional layer of wax. Thus she both reveals and conceals. She renders the marks, indentations, wrinkles, and scars on his body invisible, yet preserves them at the same time. Initially Kher wanted to treat the figures of her parents in the same way, only to find that this was simply not possible: "Then I felt, I could never know this body. It is easier to know your mother. You have been inside your mother and so perhaps fathers are more difficult to unpack. So I made a hole to see inside."[12]

"Thus this vegetal material that bees have 'digested' in their bodies and in a sense rendered organic, this material nestled against my flesh, becomes *like flesh*. This is its subtlety but also its sovereign *power*: Everything in it – plasticity, instability, fragility, sensitivity to heat, and so on – suggests the feeling or fantasy of flesh."[13]

— Georges Didi-Huberman

The hole is where the heart would be – it makes the hollowness of the sculpture more apparent. The body as house. For Kher this has also a healing aspect – healing the heart, healing a relationship. "Create space in the heart so that it becomes well."[14]

In Kher's mind there is a connection between language and materials, between material and alchemies, between wax and parenthood, since wax is one of the few materials (like mercury) that retains its original properties even when it is heated or cooled and worked and formed into different shapes.[15] "Interesting then to define this idea of parenthood – two things can be different – mother and father – and yet they can represent the same singular unit. It's a kind of symbiosis, a unity that creates this somatic cell nuclear transfer where two entities become a single moment of contact that becomes you and then a being."[16]

"But even as I speak, I put the wax by the fire and look:
the shape is lost, the size increases; it becomes liquid
and hot; you can hardly touch it, and if you strike it,
it no longer makes a sound. But does the same wax
remain? It must be admitted that it does; no one denies
it, no one thinks otherwise. So what was it in the wax that
I understood with such distinctness? Evidently none of
the features which I arrive at by means of the senses;
for whatever came under taste, smell, sight, touch or
hearing has now altered – yet the wax remains. . . .
I must therefore conclude that the nature of this piece
of wax is in no way revealed by my imagination, but is
perceived by the mind alone."[17]

— René Descartes

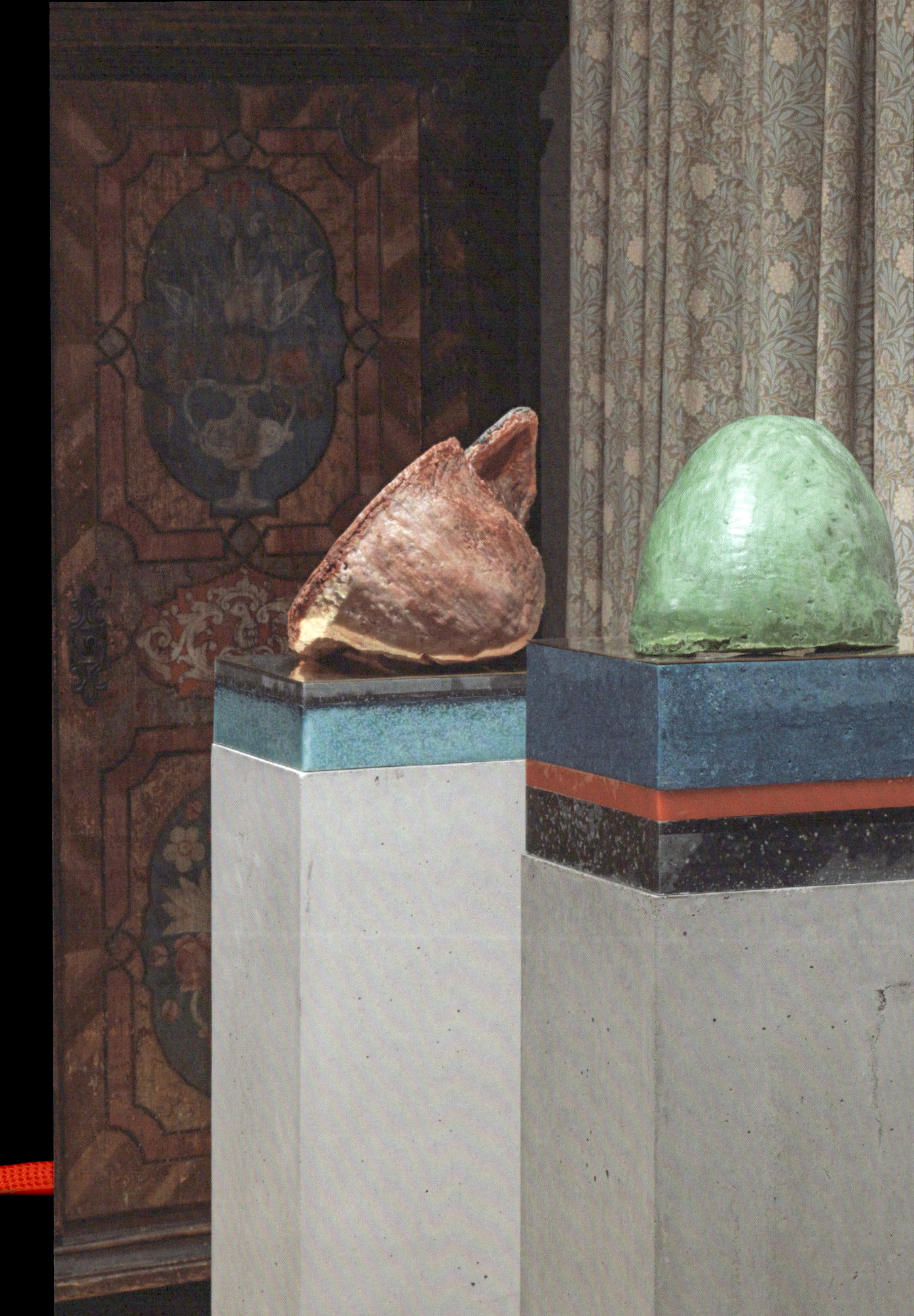

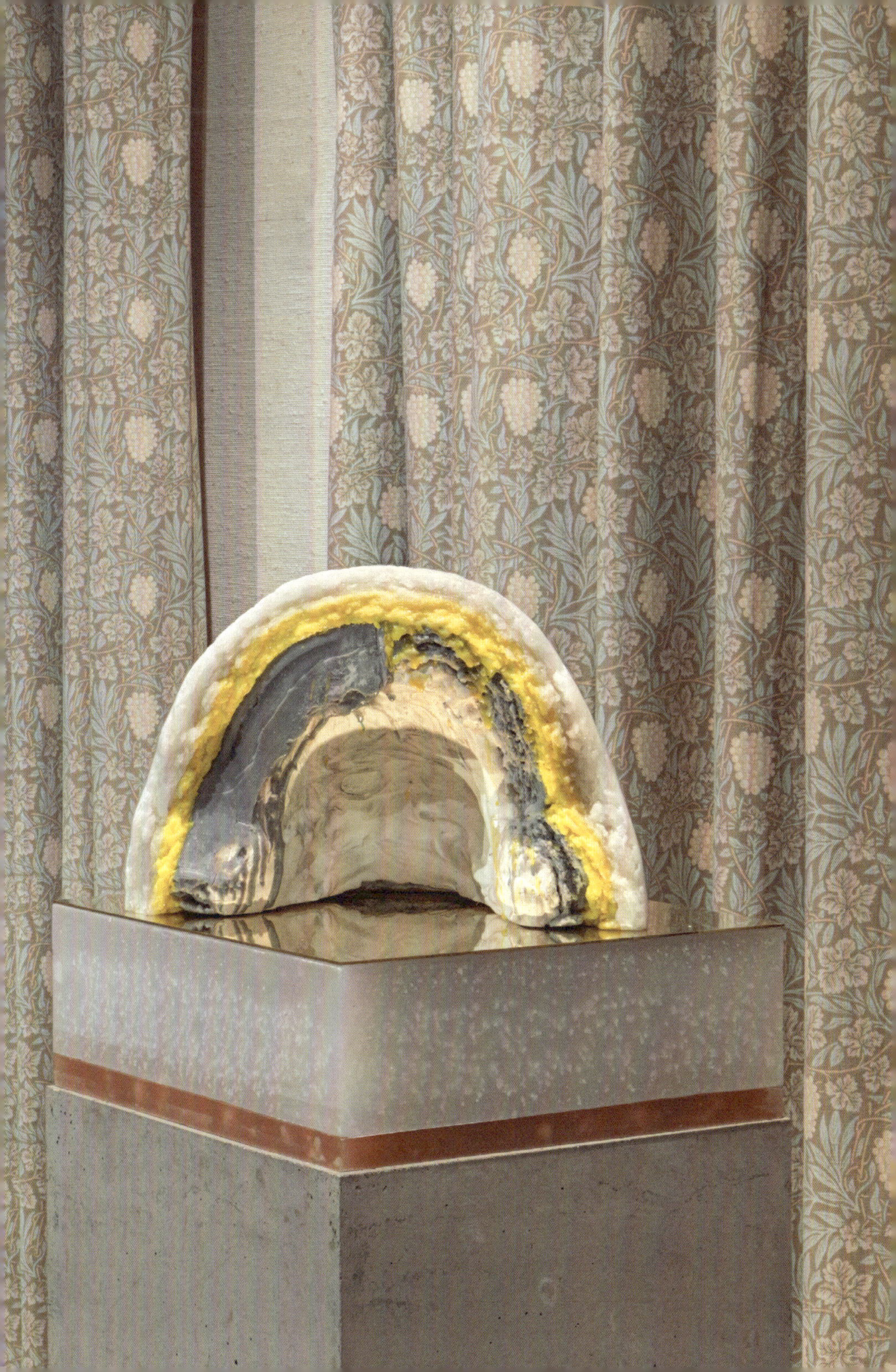

7.

Heads

"A genetic chimerism or chimera (also spelled chimaera)
is a single organism composed of cells from different
zygotes. This can result in male and female organs, two
blood types, or subtle variations in form. Animal chimeras
are produced by the merger of multiple fertilised eggs.
In plant chimeras, however, the distinct types of tissue
may originate from the same zygote, and the difference
is often due to mutation during ordinary cell division.
Normally, genetic chimerism is not visible on casual
inspection; however, it has been detected in the course
of proving parentage."[18]

— Wikipedia

Kher's *Chimera* – sculptures made from wax, concrete, plaster, hessian
fibre and brass – take up and advance the idea of conserving, preserving
and archiving items.

"How often in my private mind, have I choreographed
ribbons of black and red in water, two serious ropes of
heart and mind. The ink and the blood in the turquoise
water: these are the colours inside the fucking."[19]

— Maggie Nelson

The heads are presented on concrete plinths. Their faces are lost under layers of solid wax; no longer recognisable, not exposed to any viewer's curious gaze, they have turned their faces inwards, into the form, into the wax. Kher allows faces to disappear, thus preserving and protecting them. At the same time she relies on their auratic bearing on the visitor's emotional response when he/she comes upon a face frozen in time.[20] One can penetrate ever further into them, as though one were entering a cave. They also function like time capsules, containing within them the code for their genetic information.[21]

"There probably exists no other substance that can imitate with such polyvalence both the *external flesh*, the skin, and all the *internal flesh*, the muscles and viscera which are also our flesh, but which in general are felt, seen, and touched as though they were violently heterogeneous to the integuments or the more civilized surfaces of our bodies. As shown, for example, in the celebrated Freudian dream of 'Irma's injection,' the vision of the internal flesh often appears as an anxious insight, the inverse of the human form, the formless itself."[22]

— Georges Didi-Huberman

"You take the first imprint of the skin and then you freeze it and then you cover it. It is a time capsule or the possibility of surprise when you excavate preserved bones or remains from an animal/human from 300,000 years ago. You encase something with a second material to preserve it."[23]

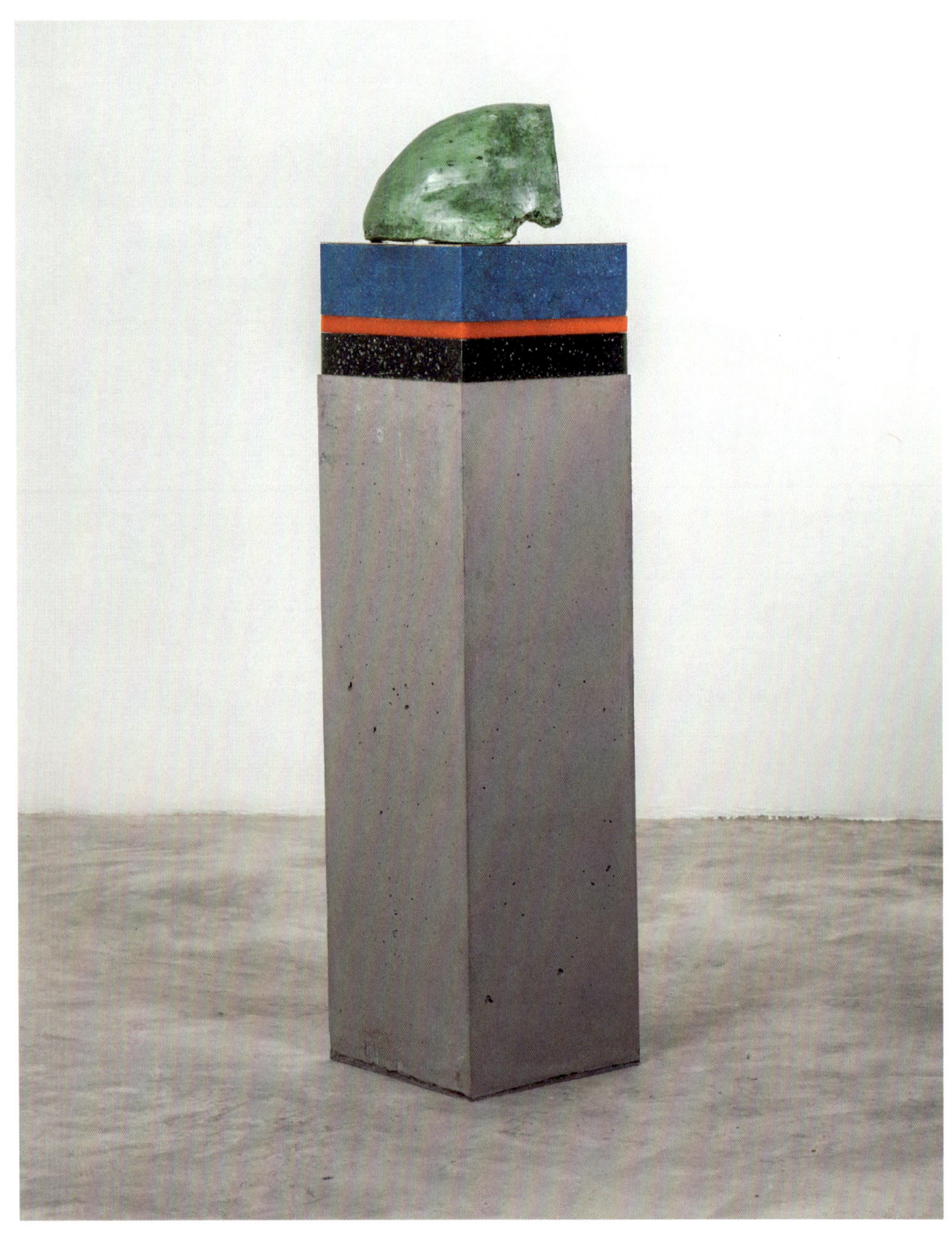

The Chimera (1), 2016
Wax, concrete, plaster, hessian fibre, brass
124.5 × 29 × 29 cm

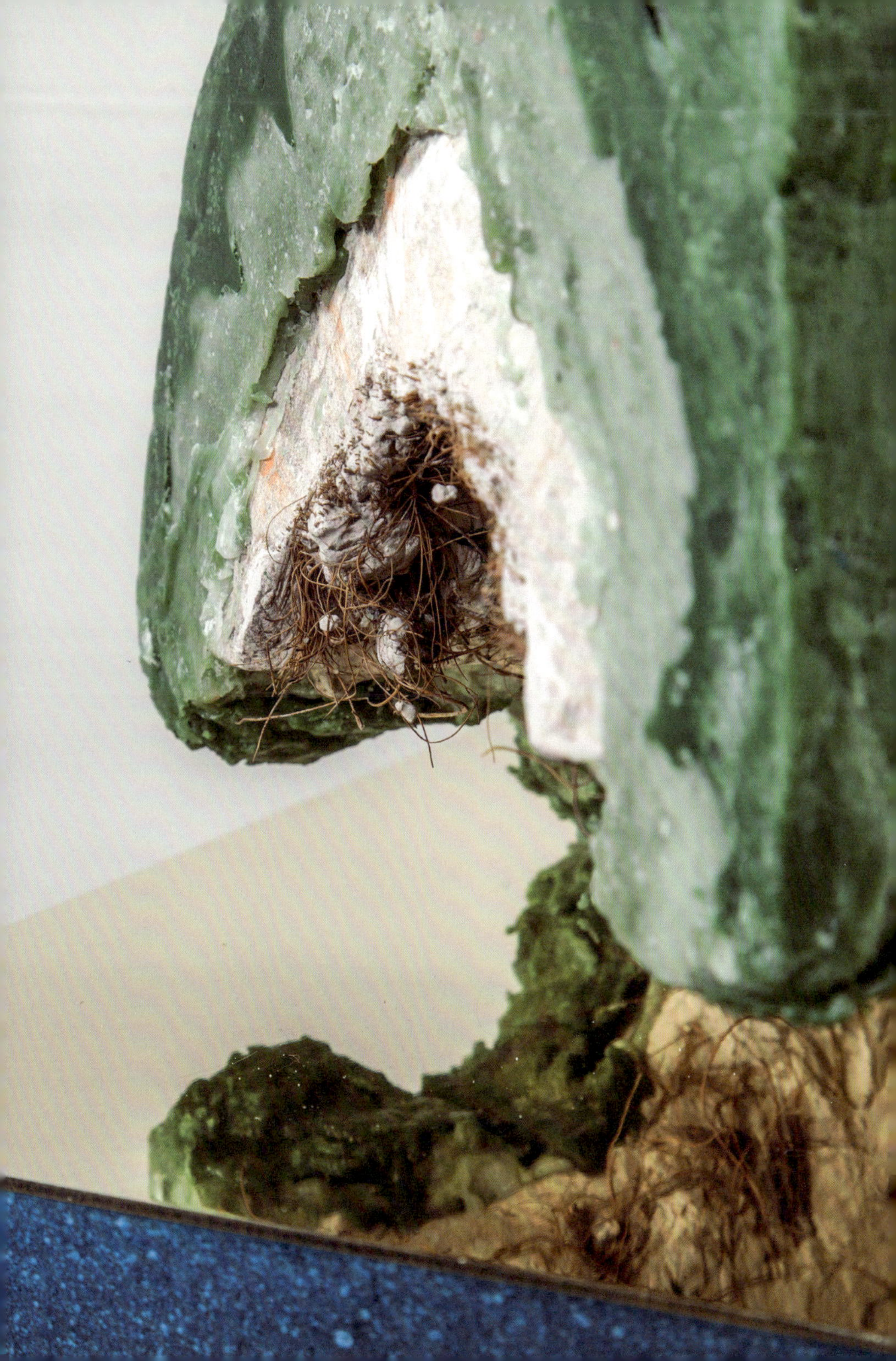

8.

Archaeology

"But these questions, in turn, raise another question,
which would identify the very archaeology of this link
between 'archaeological' and 'mortifying', between
proximity to the origin and putting the origin to death."[24]

— Georges Didi-Huberman

9.

Afterlife / Survival

"...an impurity directly connected with the process of
making a replica (in the form of a cast)...This impurity
suddenly revealed in the expressive beauty and modernism
of the faces painted by Ghirlandaio, the cold plaster of
Roman funerary masks, the fired clay of the Etruscans
and the wax, votive figures of the Middle Ages. These
different eras jostled with each other, contradicting each
other like the diverse signs in the images from which
Warburg – at a far remove from the overly peaceable
'iconological tradition' that we owe to him – would derive
a new model of temporality, a contemporary model close
to the version developed by Freud: a complex model of
what he referred to as 'Nachleben' ['afterlife', 'survival']."[25]

— Georges Didi-Huberman

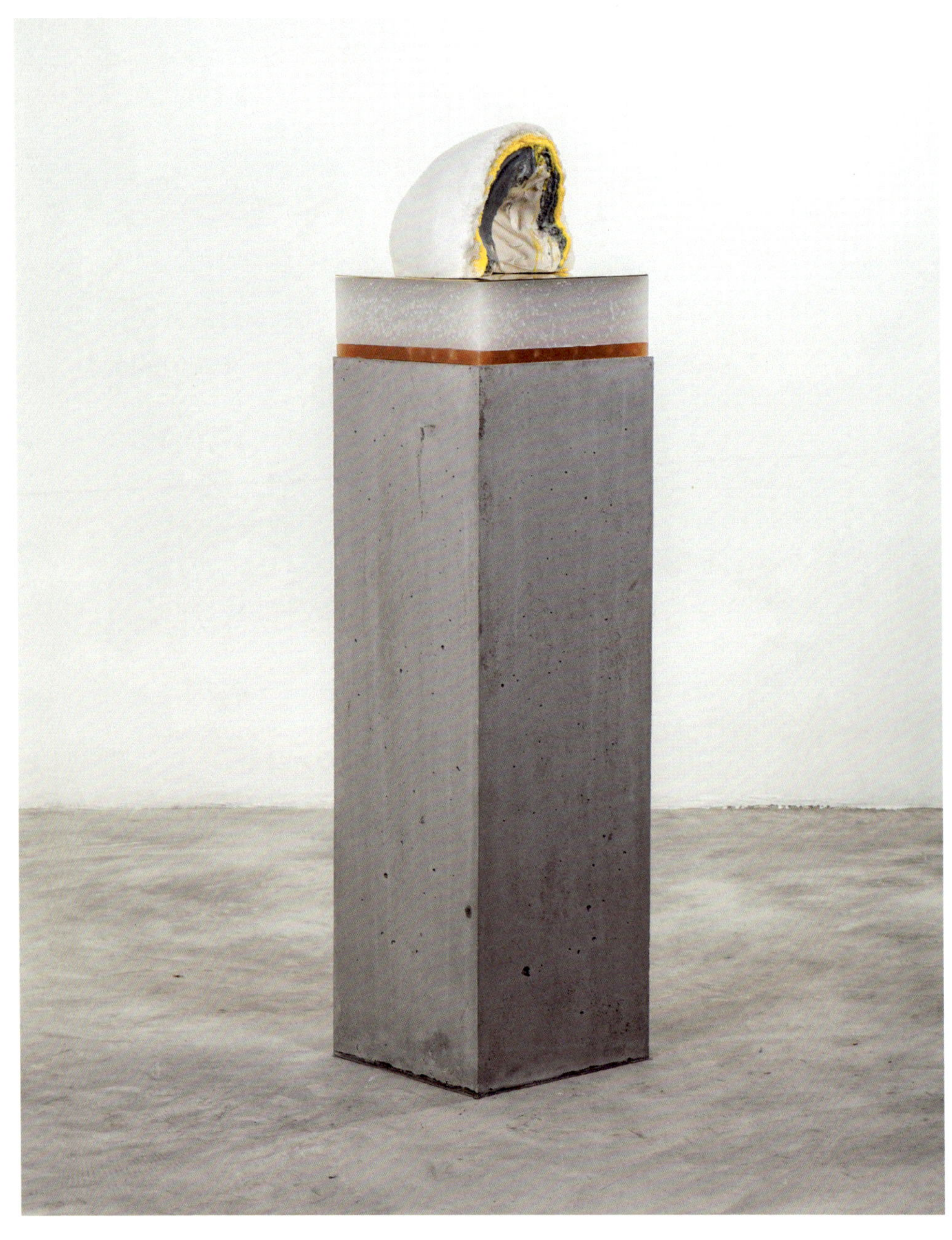

The Chimera (2), 2016
Wax, concrete, plaster, hessian fibre, brass
132×26×24 cm

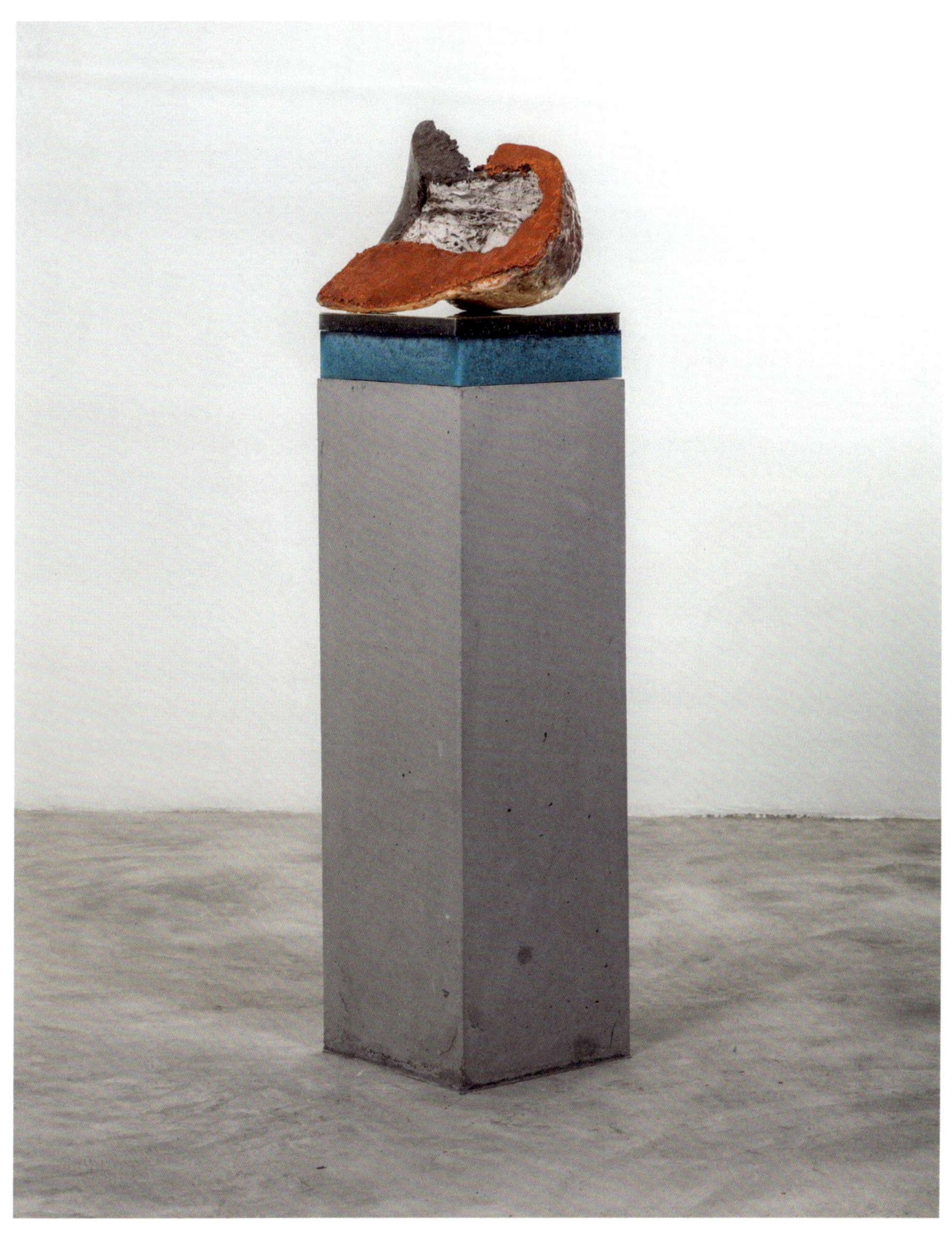

The Chimera (3), 2016
Wax, concrete, plaster, hessian fibre, brass
116×29×29 cm

10.

Mirrors

The seven-part mirror work *What can I tell you that you don't know already? II* hung in the 2nd floor hallway.

"Is the mirror's representation of us a means of self-knowledge or self-delusion? The mirror is ultimately tied to that questioning ambivalence of knowing and not knowing what it is to be a human."[26] . . . "When you experience the mirrors, I want you to get a sense of the essence of an artwork, which is that you walk into a space and you are transformed into another place or axis and perhaps for that very short moment, time will stand still for you."[27]

"The mirror also relates to the *Abwesen* ['absent-being']. Zhuangzi's empty mirror differs radically from Leibniz's animate mirror: it possesses no exi gential interiority, no 'appetition'. It seeks nothing, clings to nothing. It is empty and absent. And in this way it lets those things that are reflected in it come and go. It goes *along*, it does not go *towards*. And so it also doesn't *go by*. 'The highest human being uses his heart like a mirror.'" . . . "He does not pursue things and does not go to meet them; he reflects them but does not hold on to them . . . he is not a lord (zhu) of cognition. He takes notice of the smallest thing and is yet inexhaustible and resides beyond the self."[28]

— Byung-Chul Han

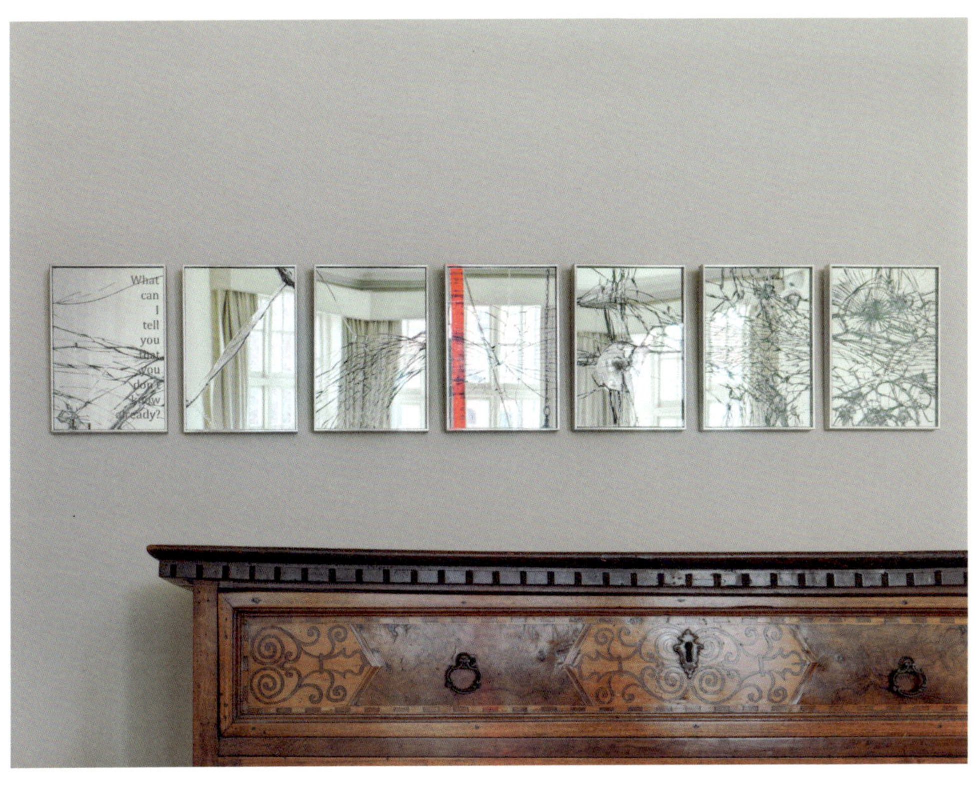

What
can
I
tell
you
that
you
don't
know
already?

What can I tell you that you don't know already? II (detail), 2013
Mirrors, resin, aluminium
29.7 × 21 cm each, 7 parts

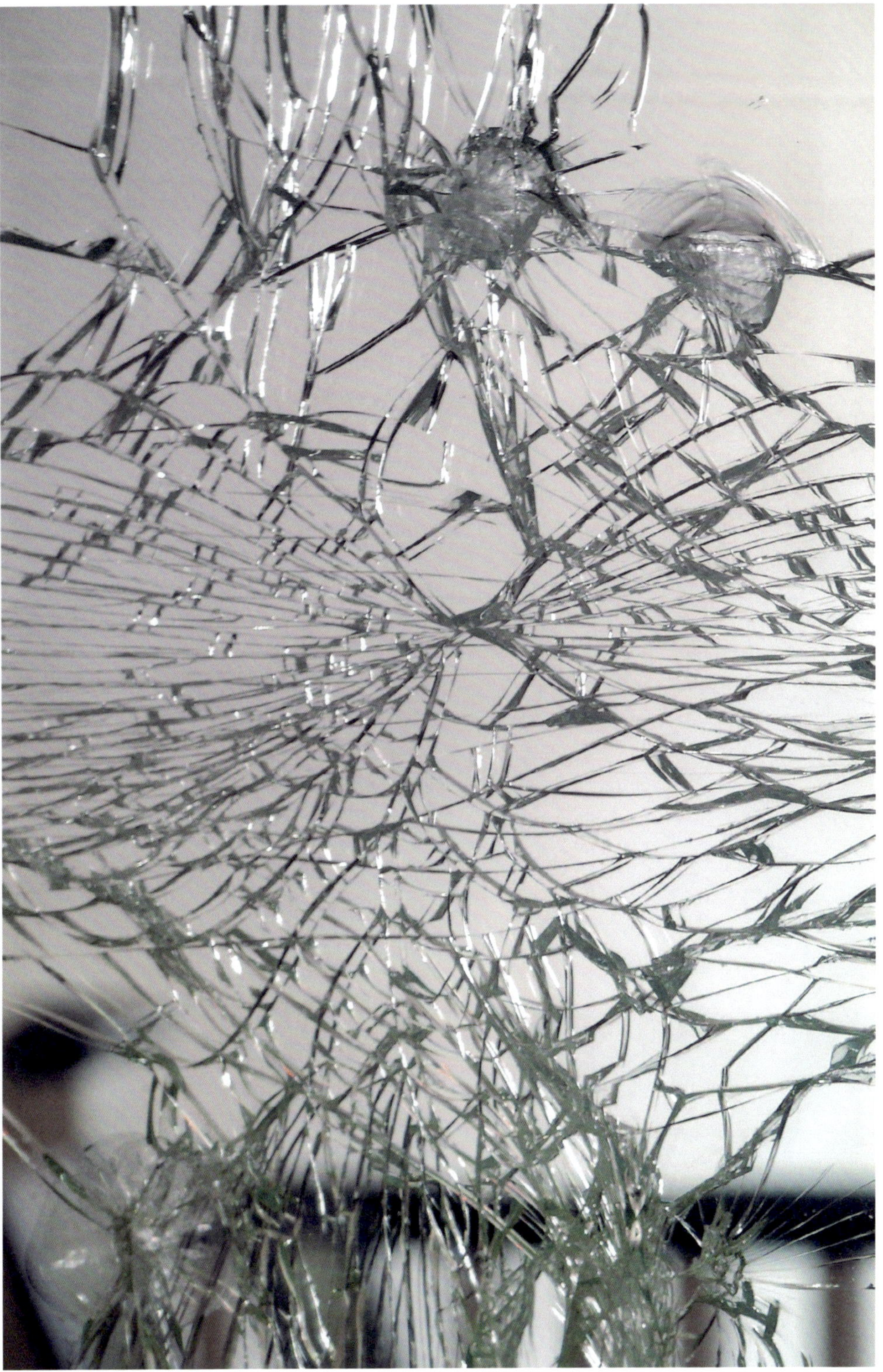

Bloodline, 2000
Acrylic, glass bangles, LED lights, stainless steel
Height variable, diameter 7 cm

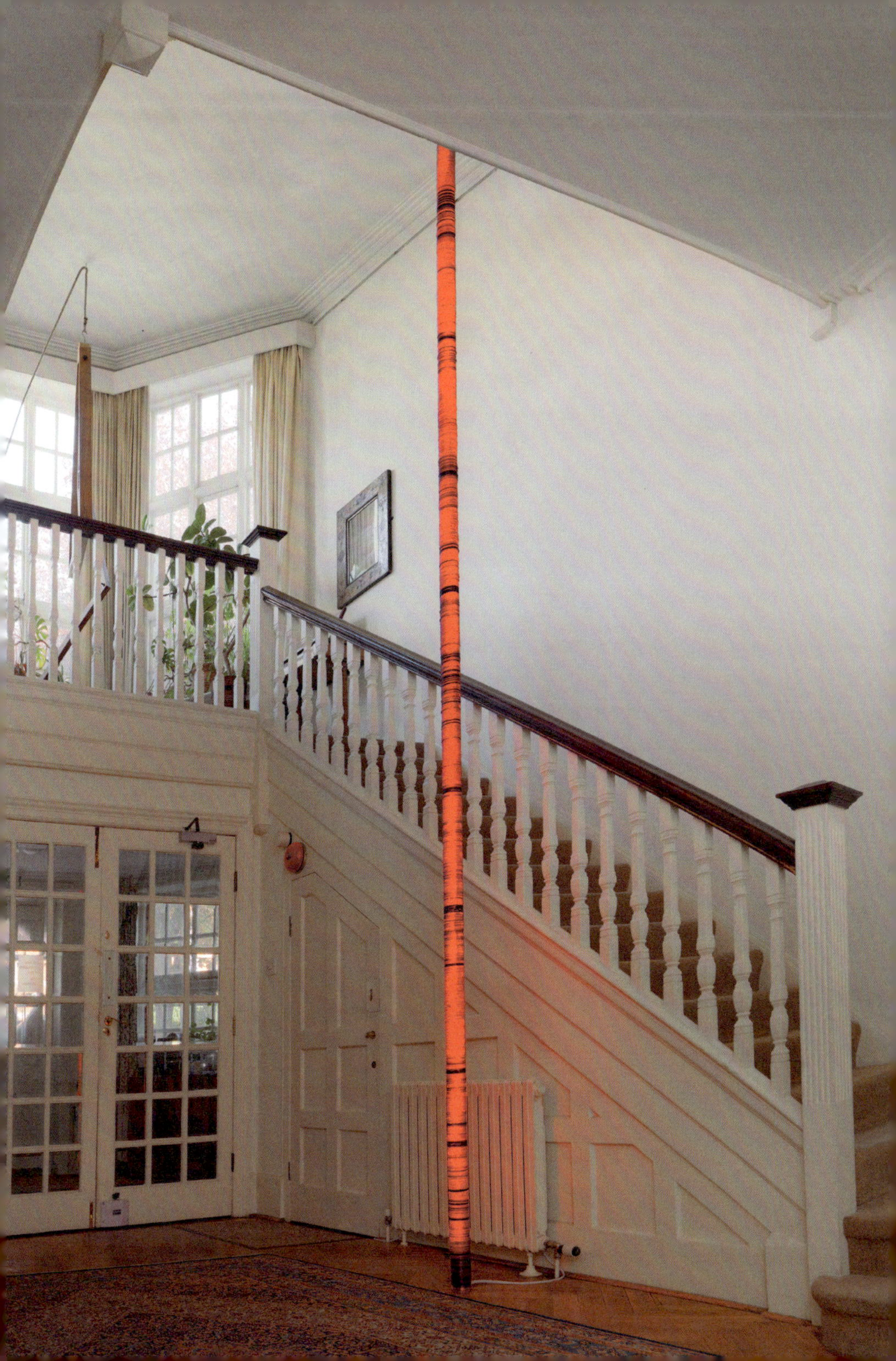

11.

Inner Space

"When we dream of the house we were born in, in the utmost depth of revery, we participate in this original warmth, in this well-tempered matter of the material paradise. This is the environment in which the protective beings live. We shall come back to the maternal features of the house. For the moment, I should like to point out the original fullness of the house's being."[29]

— Gaston Bachelard

House and body, body and studio seem to be interchangeable here. Perhaps they can be equated with Kher's own *ur*-house,[30] whose internal workings she has been exploring in her art.[31]

"The house, quite obviously, is a privileged entity for a phenomenological study of the intimate values of inside space, provided, of course, that we take it in both its unity and its complexity, and endeavour to integrate all the special values in one fundamental value."[32]

— Gaston Bachelard

Kher pumps blood and life through the building. *Bloodline* (made from clinking, red glass bangles of the kind traditionally worn by women in India) is both the backbone and main artery of the building.

Equilibrium – a wooden triangle – marks the central core of the house; it is the solar plexus and reminds the viewer of the fundamental need for balance.[33] "Even referring to a state of psychology. We are all so close to tipping at any given point, that we constantly seek a kind of balance. But the triangles, they hold the time."[34] "The point of contact and balance is a point that marks the place and time and coordinates of where the world can stand still for a minute of a second of a degree."[35]

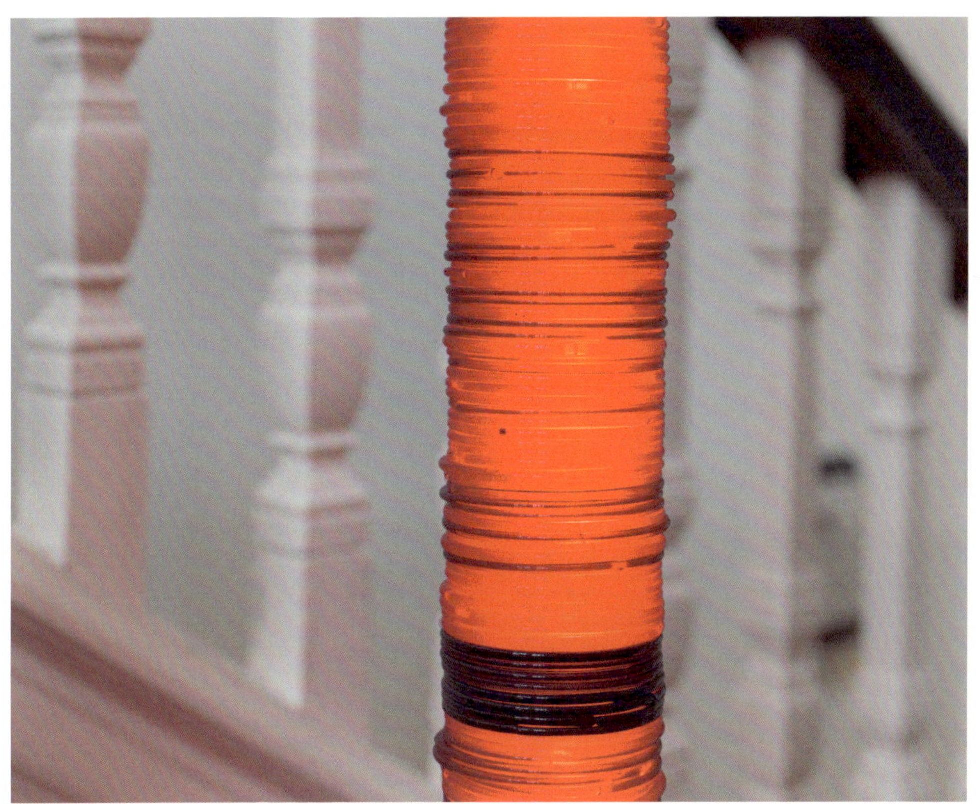

12.

A Triangle

"A triangle truly embodies contradiction. If you experience shape, you can feel clearly an inside space and an outside one. It's intrinsic to how we understand the world, specifically the space we occupy as body. Circles make us feel enclosed and safe inside, squares are rudimentary and give structure to the abyss, cylinders suggest a connection from top to bottom, a linear journey. Triangles however have no inside or outside . . ."[36]

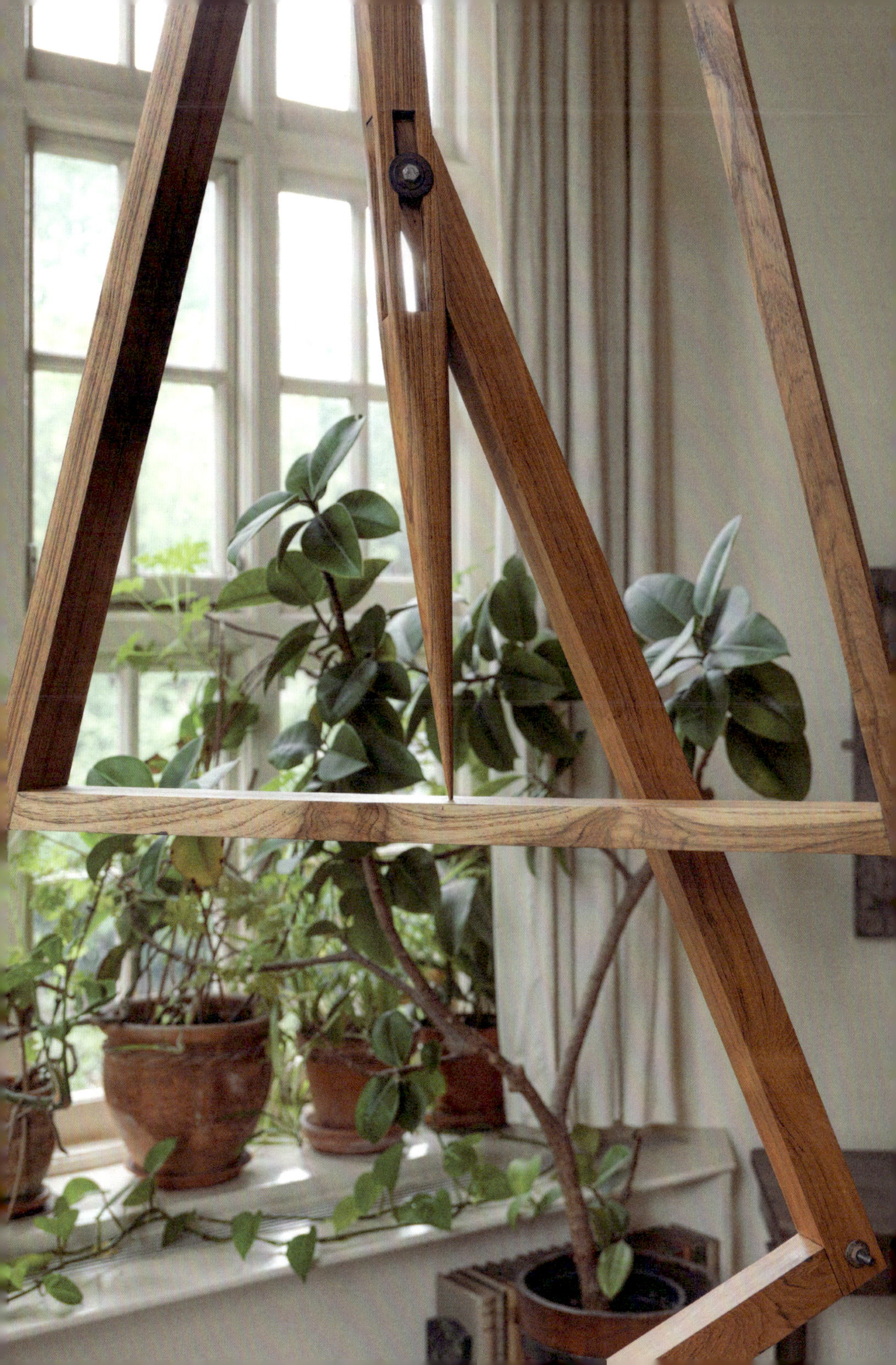

Equilibrium, 2015
Wood, steel, rope
$262 \times 153 \times 4$ cm
Installation dimensions variable

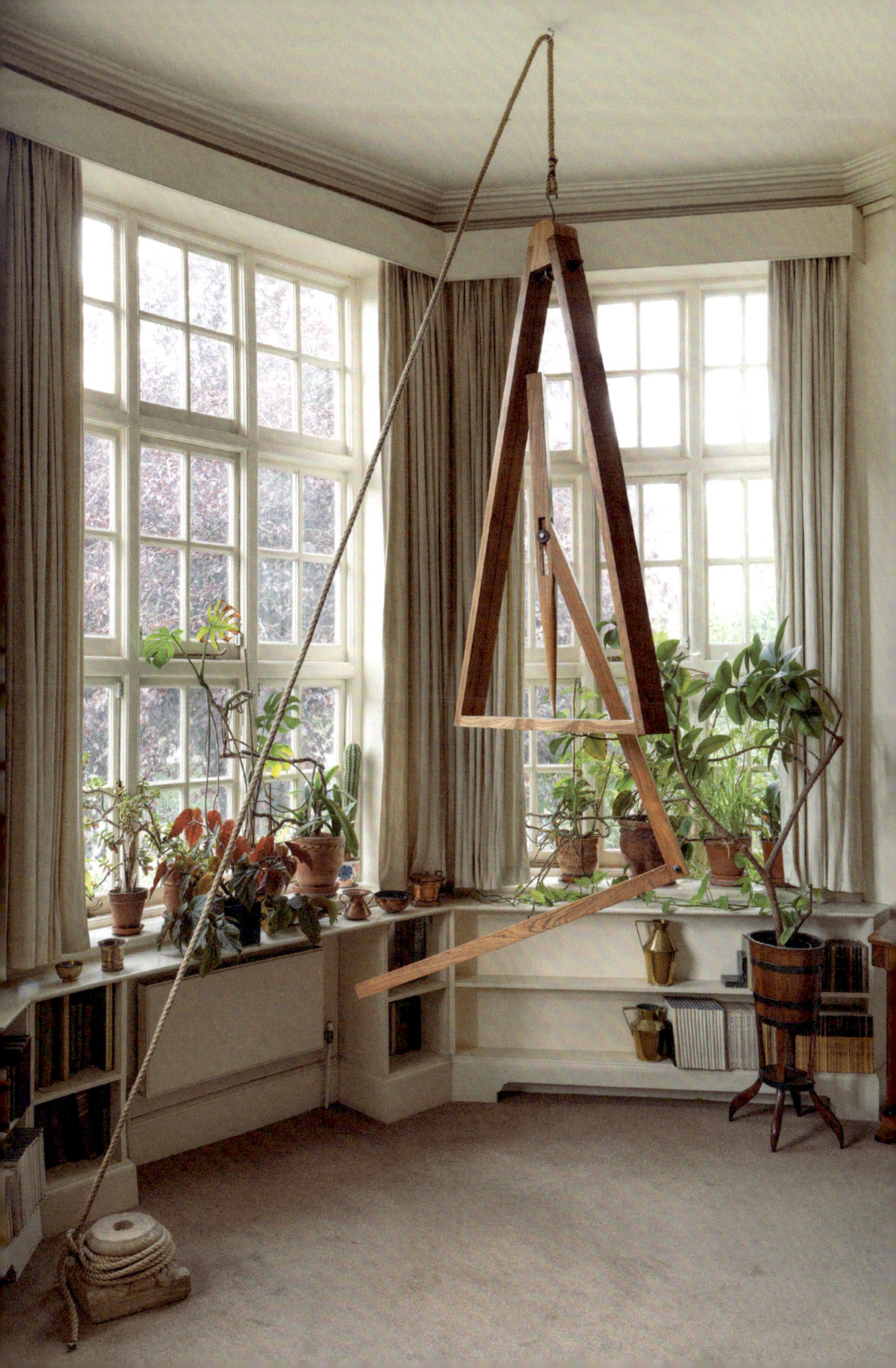

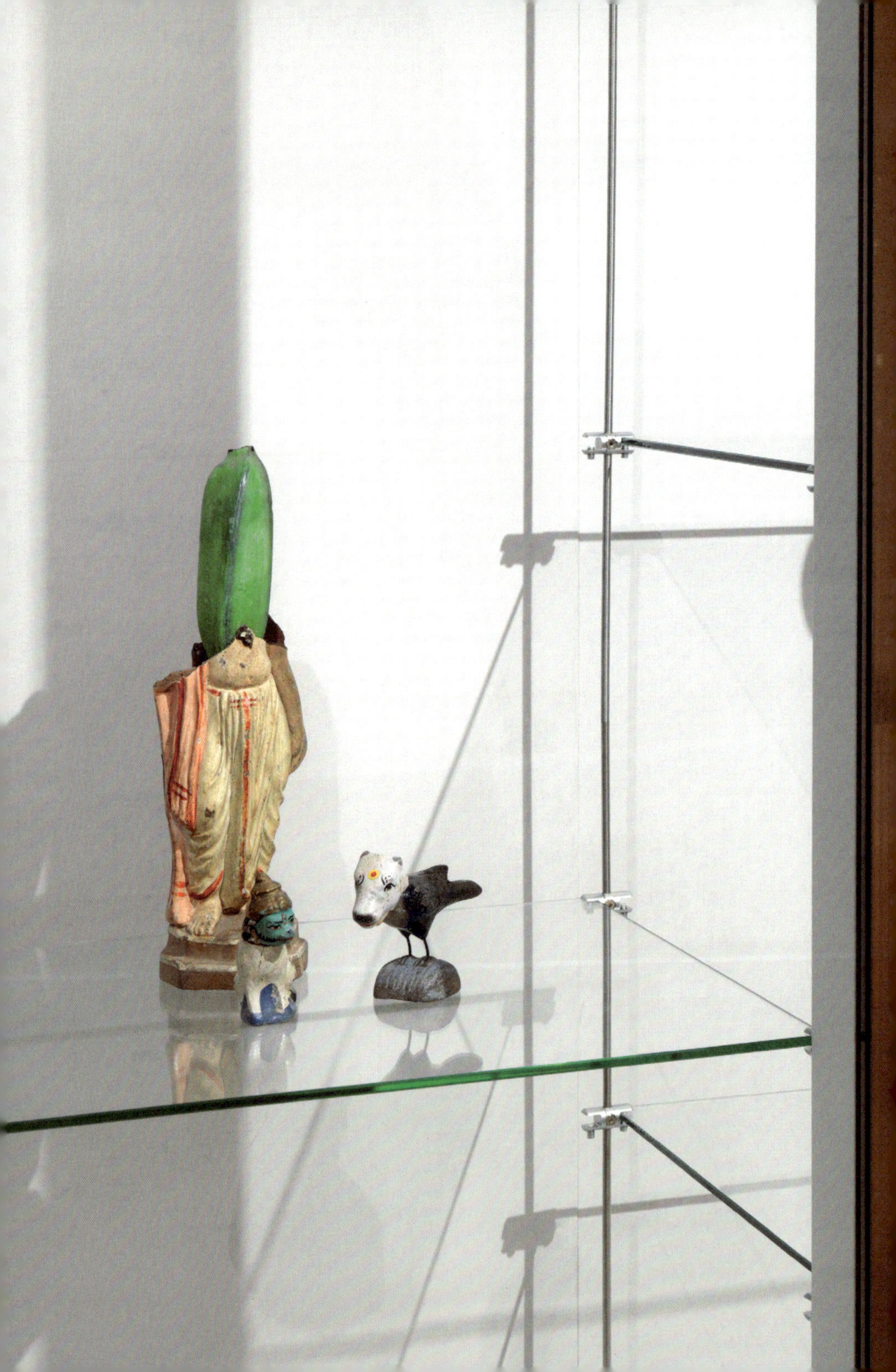

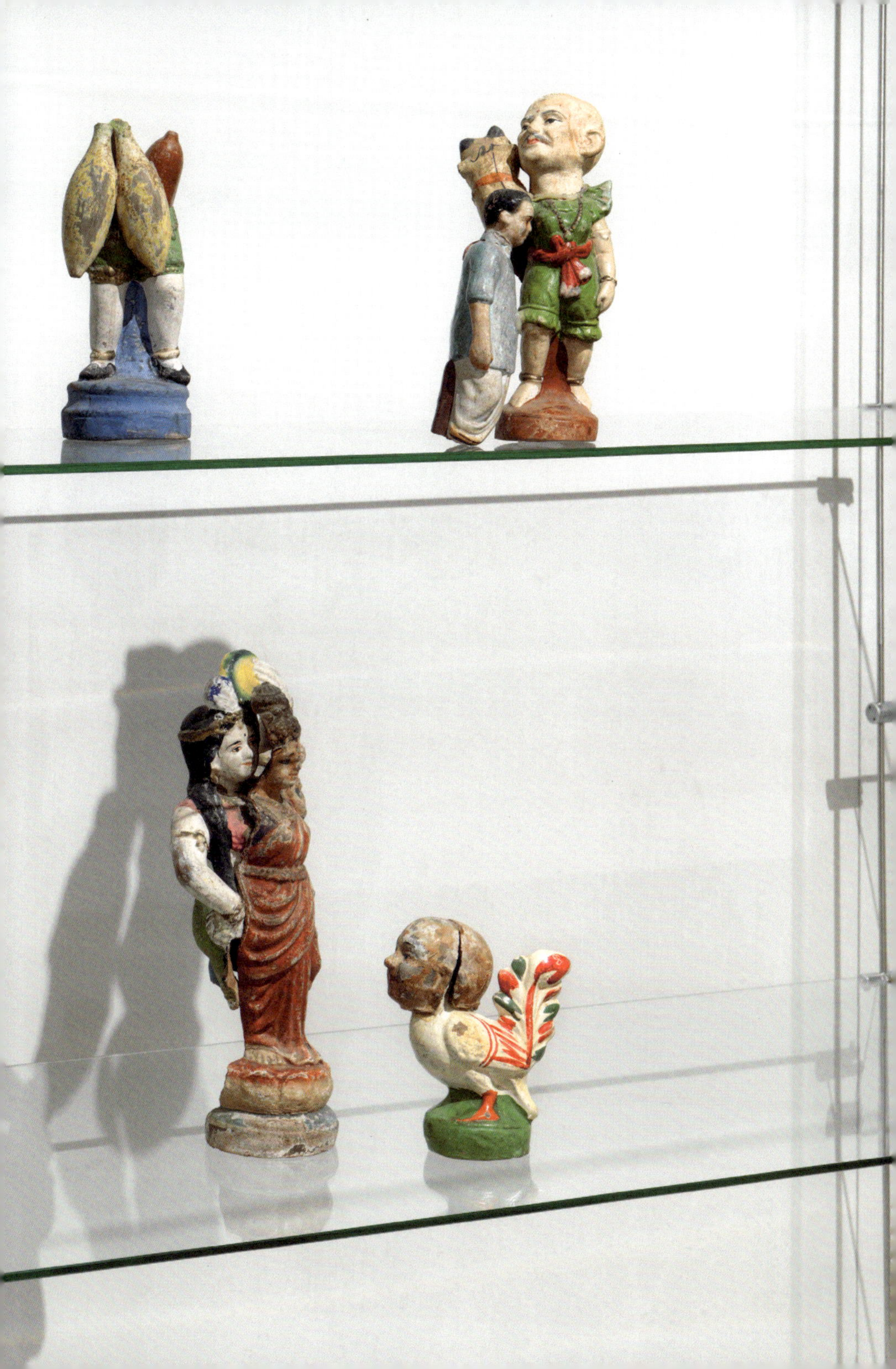

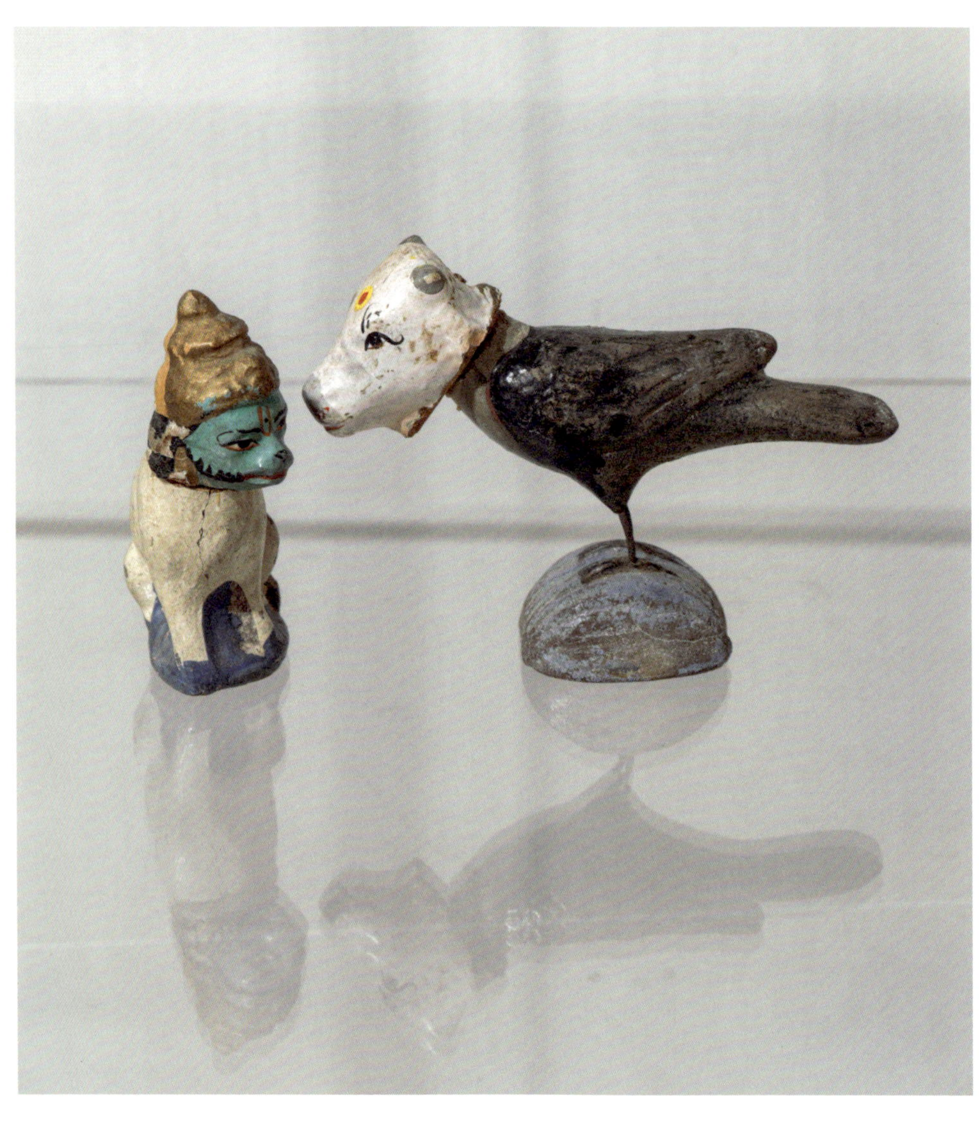

The Intermediaries (6), 2016
Clay
7 × 7 × 5 cm and 7 × 13 × 5 cm

54

13.

The Intermediaries

"The broken idols: 'The Intermediaries' are part secular and part deity. The clay sculptures are made in the south of India to be taken out once a year during festival time. They are already finished objects that take the form of people, food and the earthly. Some of them arrived broken and I began to see them as the broken idols . . . the ones that could no longer be worshipped or prayed to."[37]

These little figurines, partly broken and newly brought together look as though they are invading the building, as does the bronze breast plate[38] that Kher adds to one of the oldest sculptures from Freud's collection and as do concrete casts of her walking boots, entitled *Self-Portrait: Boots*, which find a place right next to boots once worn by Anna Freud. These works look like little growths, rampant plants that are spreading slowly but steadily. They are not malevolent, yet they do palpably disturb the viewer, as an itch might.

Throughout his life Freud was an avid collector and described his activities in this area as an addiction (his second-most important addiction after smoking). He regularly arranged a changing selection of sculptures on his desk. Little bronze, wood, and marble sculptures from Egypt, China, Greece and Rome. It was as though he were creating a small exhibition of these objects, which closely related to the texts he was writing. Yet again Kher erases, eradicates and highlights items at one and the same time.

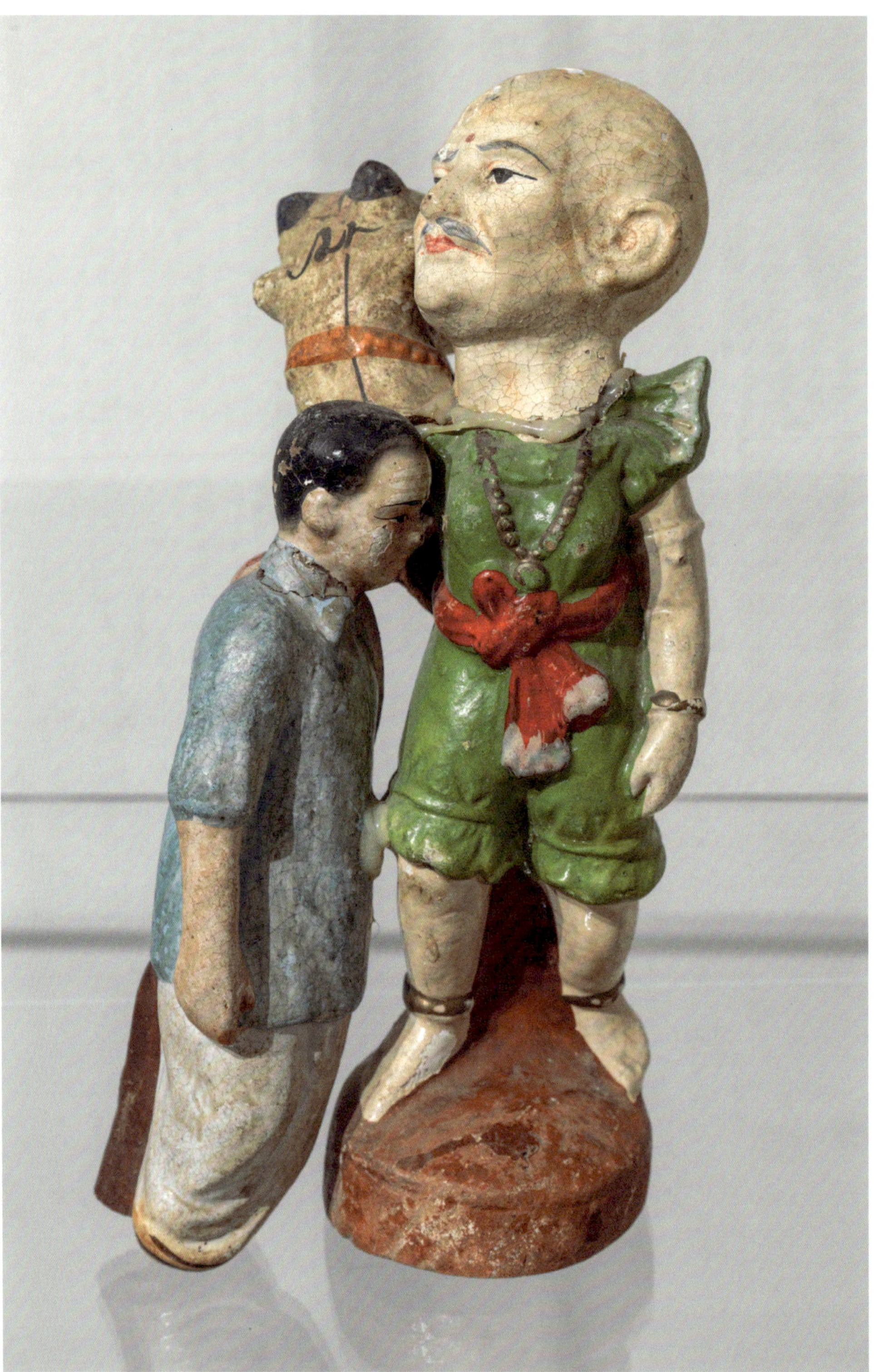

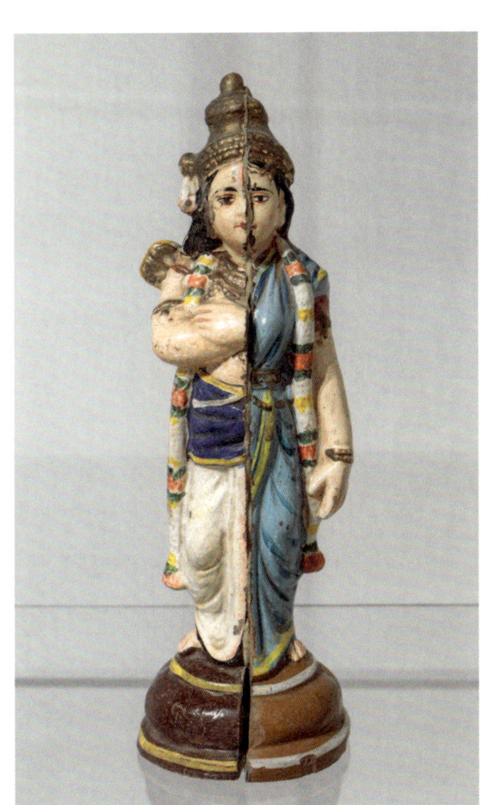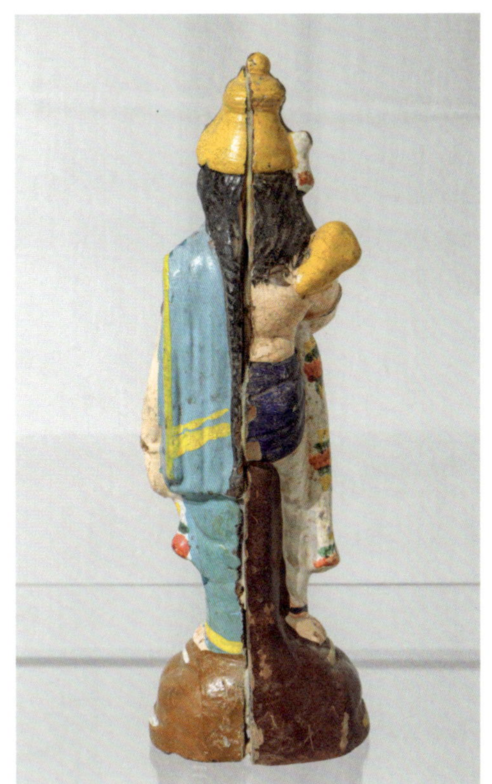

Above:
The Intermediaries (8), 2016
Clay
26 × 8 × 9 cm

Left:
The Intermediaries (7), 2016
Clay
20 × 12 × 8 cm

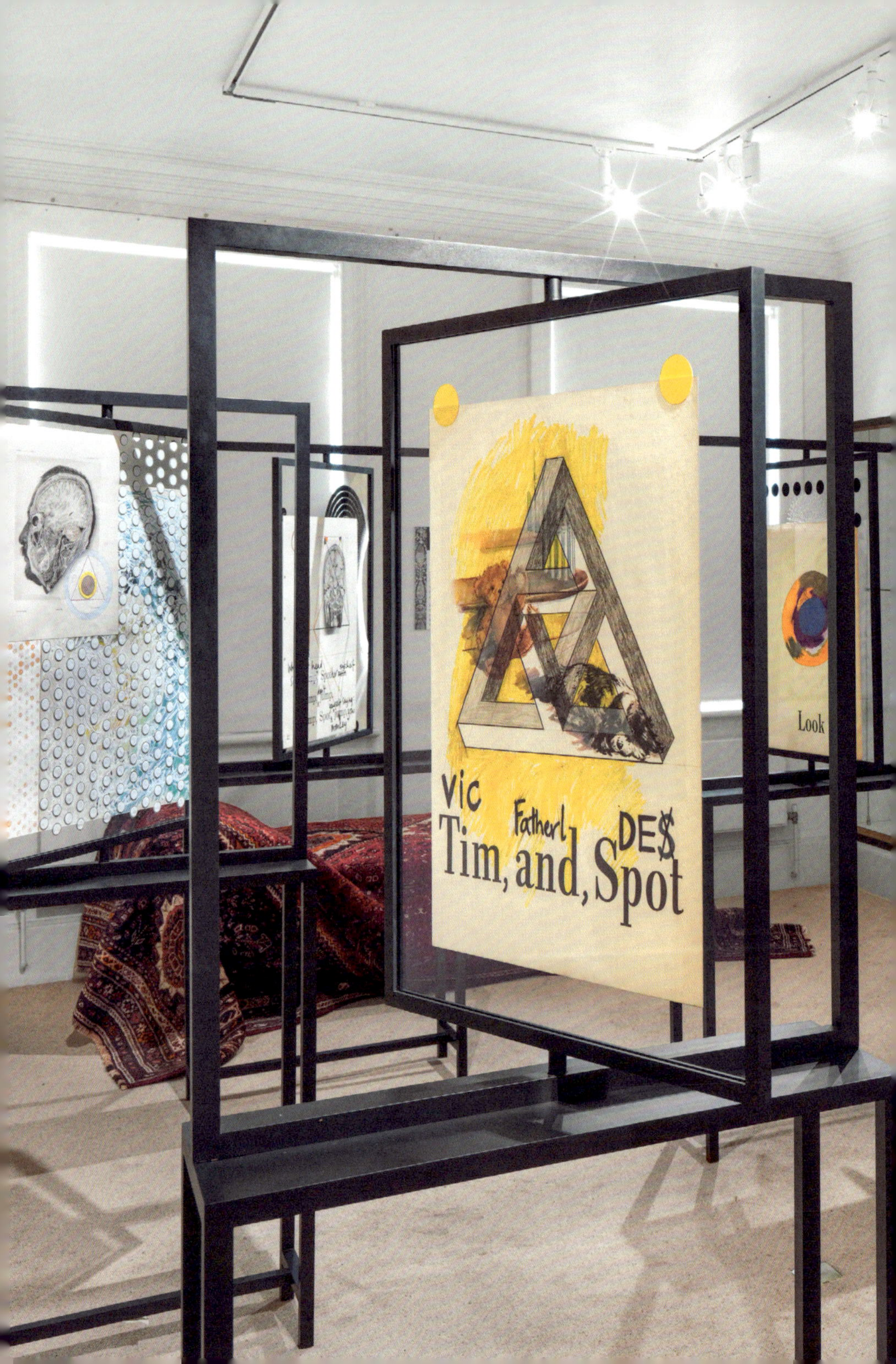

VIC
Fatherl
Tim, and, Spot
DE$
Look

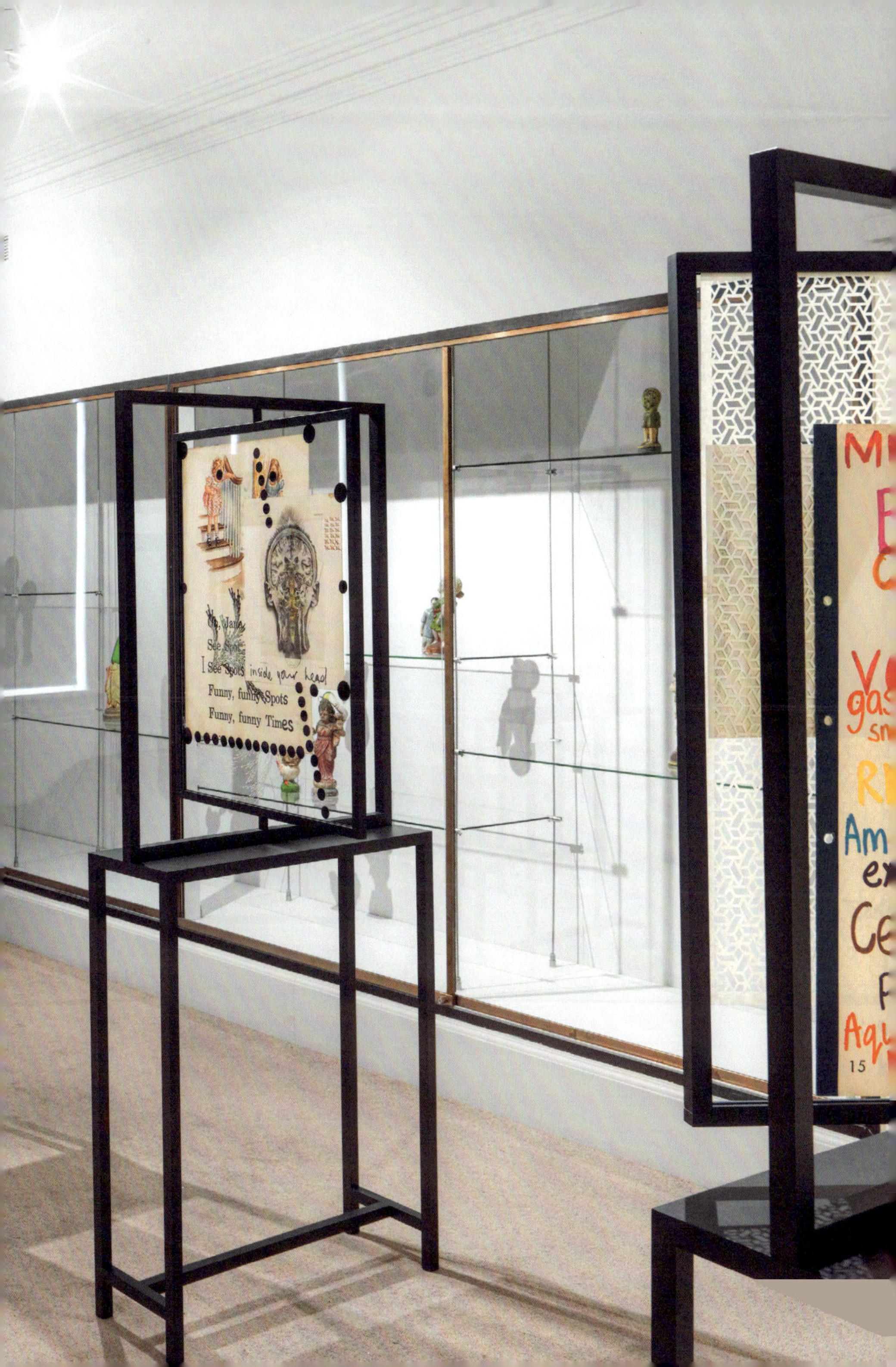
Oh, Jane
See Spot
I See Spots inside your head
Funny, funny Spots
Funny, funny Times

14.

Anxiety

"It is in the early infantile sexual period and not at puberty
that the crucial steps in development are taken, the most
important pre-genital phases of sexual organization are
passed through, the different component instincts are
developed and brought into action and the normality or
abnormality of the individual, his capacity or incapacity
for love, are determined.

In each case – in the early infantile period, at puberty,
and at the climacteric – a relatively strong id confronts
a relatively weak ego."[39]

— Anna Freud

In the exhibition *Links in a Chain* – A3-sized collages – are on display
next to Anna Freud's study, which contains influential books such as
her own *The Ego and the Mechanisms of Defence*, a treatise on the
subconscious implementation of defence mechanisms in the hope of
avoiding feelings of anxiety. The paper works connect with Kher's own
frenetic behaviour: "There is a part of me that can't actually leave –
the chattering monkey . . . which is what I call it. It's that part of your
brain that you are supposed probably to let go of. I personally need
to befriend it more first. But you also let it do its thing because it's also
very creative. So I hold on to it: my devil and my bad."[40]

The collages revolve around anxiety, hysteria, and perhaps childhood. Kher describes her collages as "let[ting] the craziness unfold" and "embracing the dark night". The collages use pages from *Sally, Dick and Jane*, a series of school textbooks for children learning to read, popular in the 1930s to the 1970s. Kher found the book in an American antiquarian bookshop in 2012. She plays with language in these collages – erasing, over-writing and adding text. She both preserves and deletes in the same moment.

The drawings are unsettling and touch a nerve in our childhood memories: "The sense that you have that thought, then a genesis of learning. All slightly awkward: the games we play, the things we learn."[41]

"They have sat in a drawer I suppose, waiting to be needed and the Freud Museum became the activator for the prints. They work well I think, with the development of the child and how reading then becomes a door to the next stage of life from, say, the age of 5 or 6. And what Freud called the Phallic Stage/Electra Complex from say 3 to 6 years. Innocence and brutality, love, need and desire somehow all walk together throughout our lives. We watch as our children play adult games."[42]

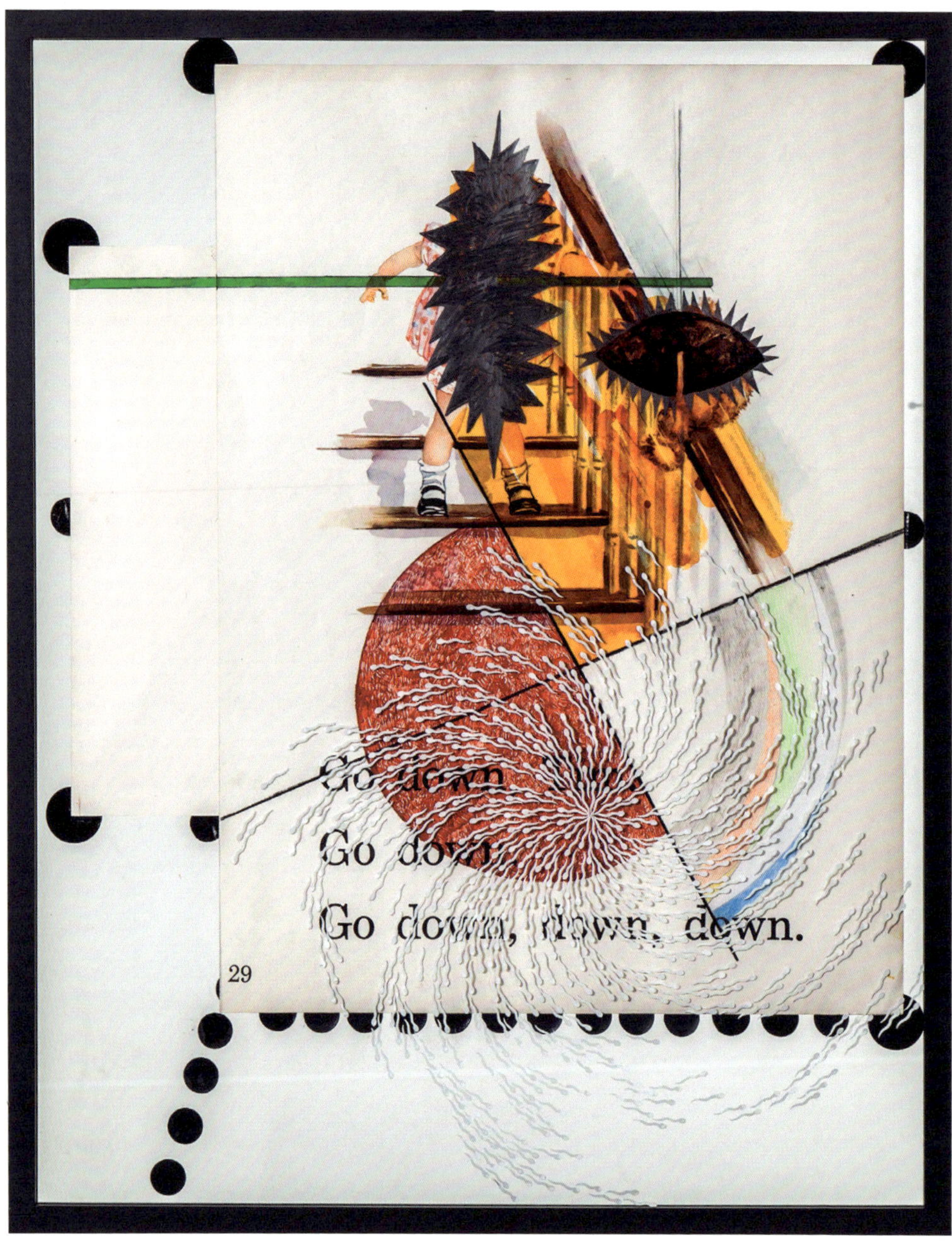

Links in a Chain (1) (detail), 2016
Mixed media
182 × 72.5 × 25 cm

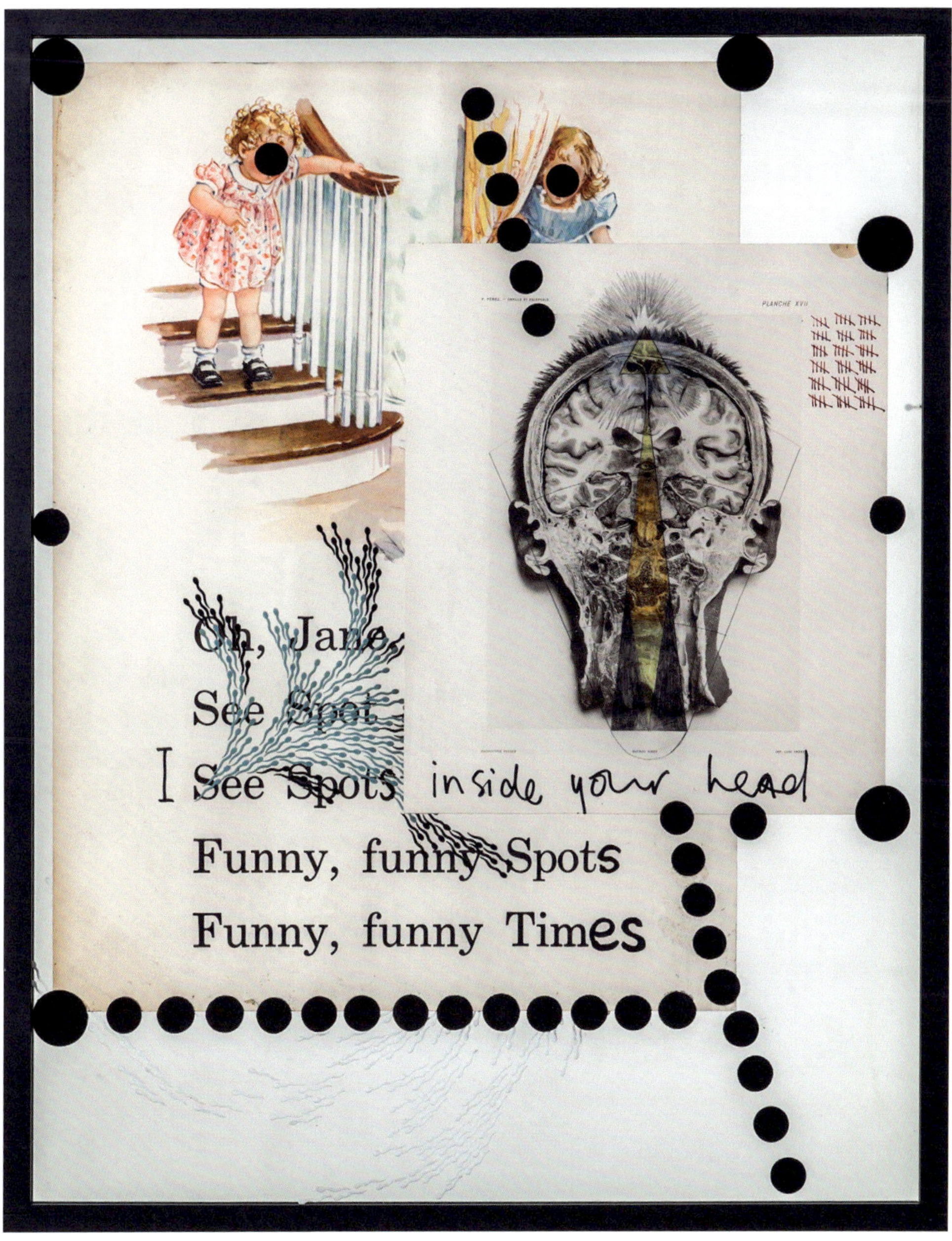

Links in a Chain (1) (detail), 2016
Mixed media
182 × 72.5 × 25 cm

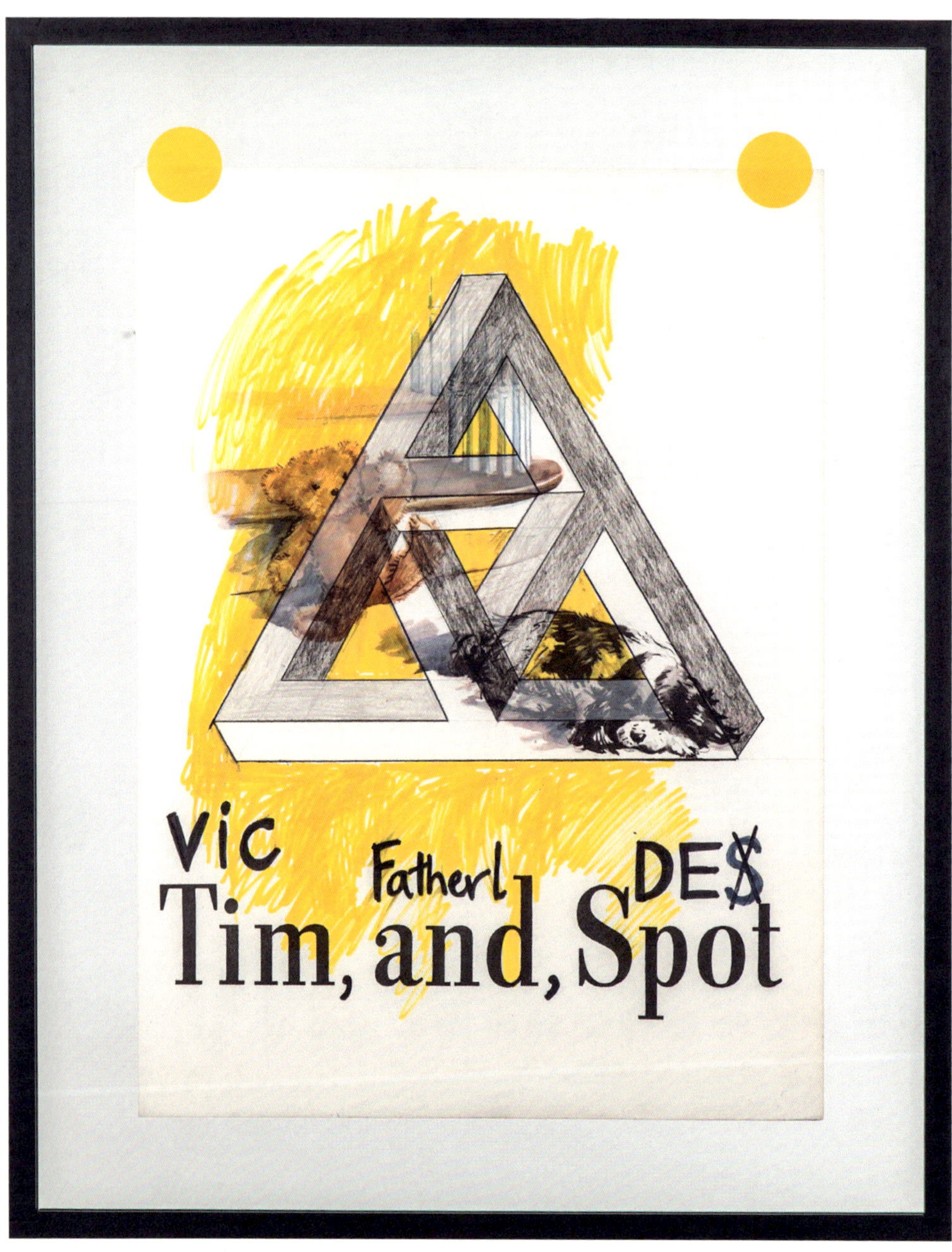

Links in a Chain (2) (detail), 2016
Mixed media
182 × 72.5 × 25 cm

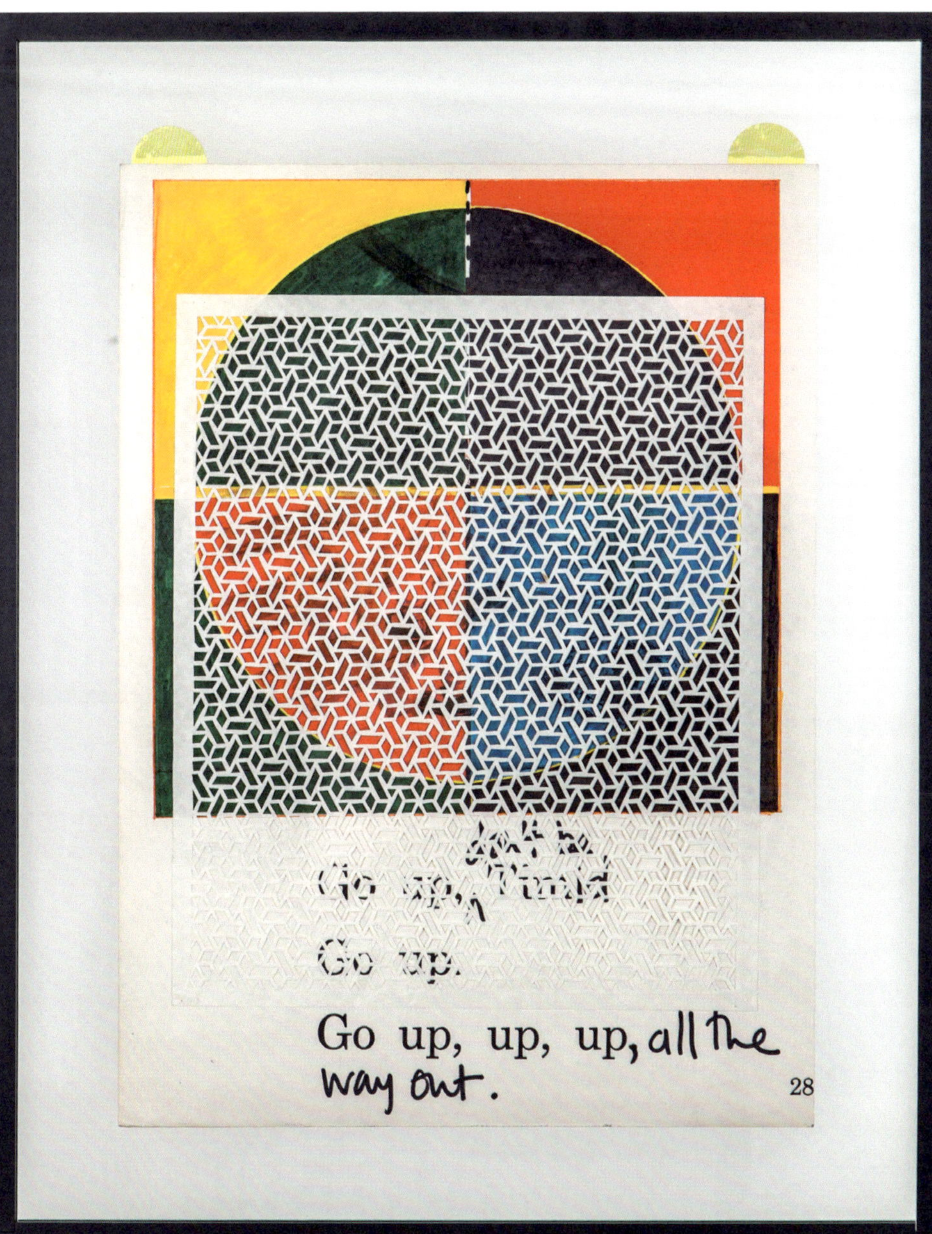

Links in a Chain (2) (detail), 2016
Mixed media
182 × 72.5 × 25 cm

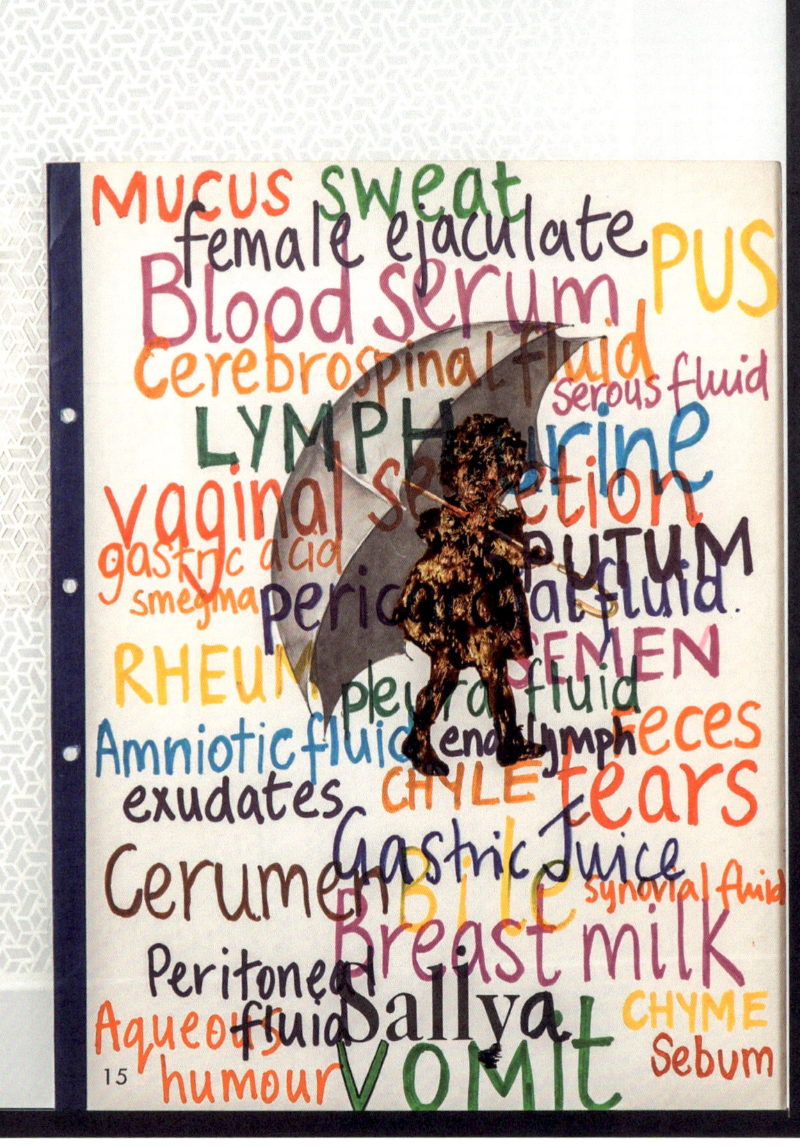

Links in a Chain (3) (detail), 2016
Mixed media
182 × 72.5 × 25 cm

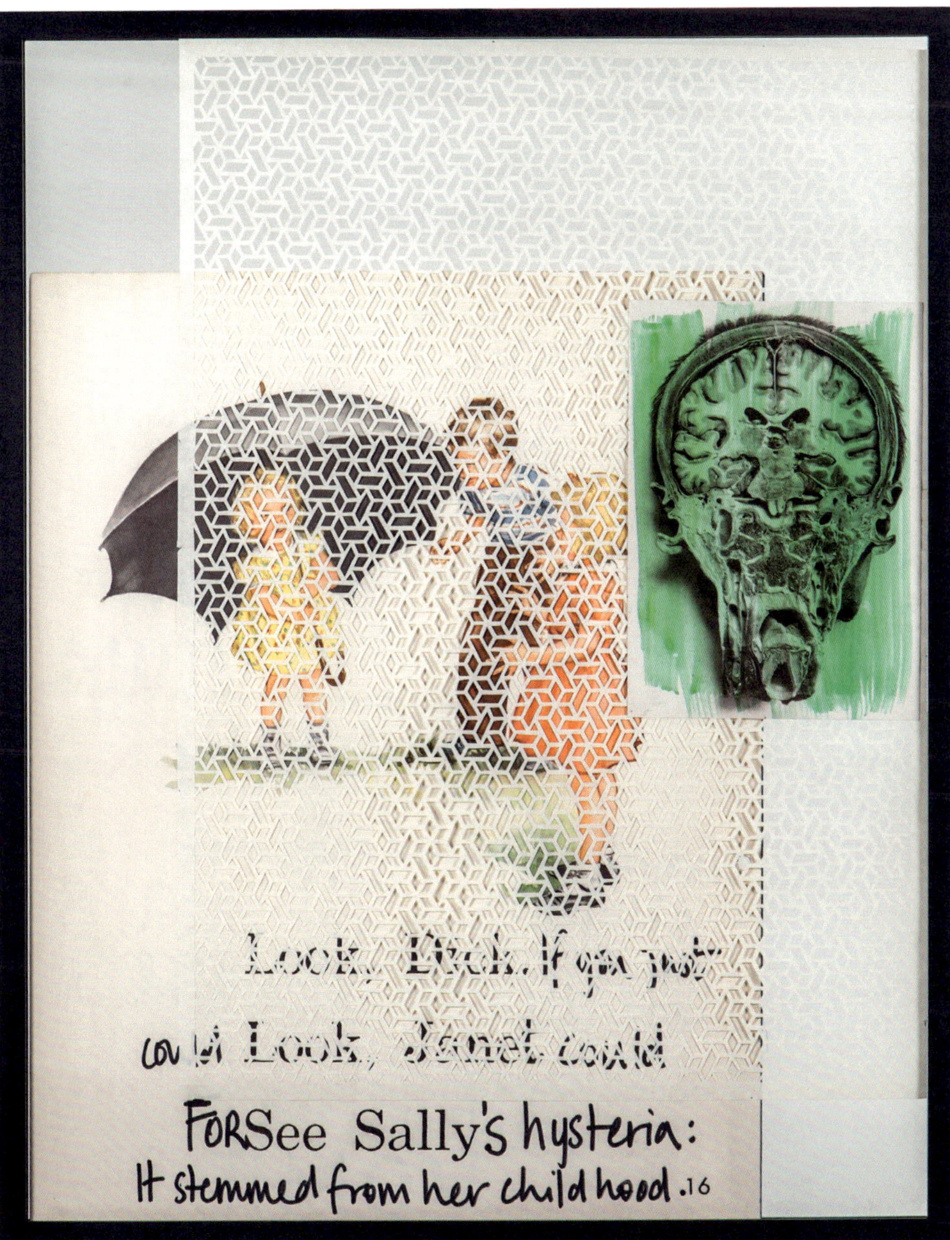

Links in a Chain (3) (detail), 2016
Mixed media
182 × 72.5 × 25 cm

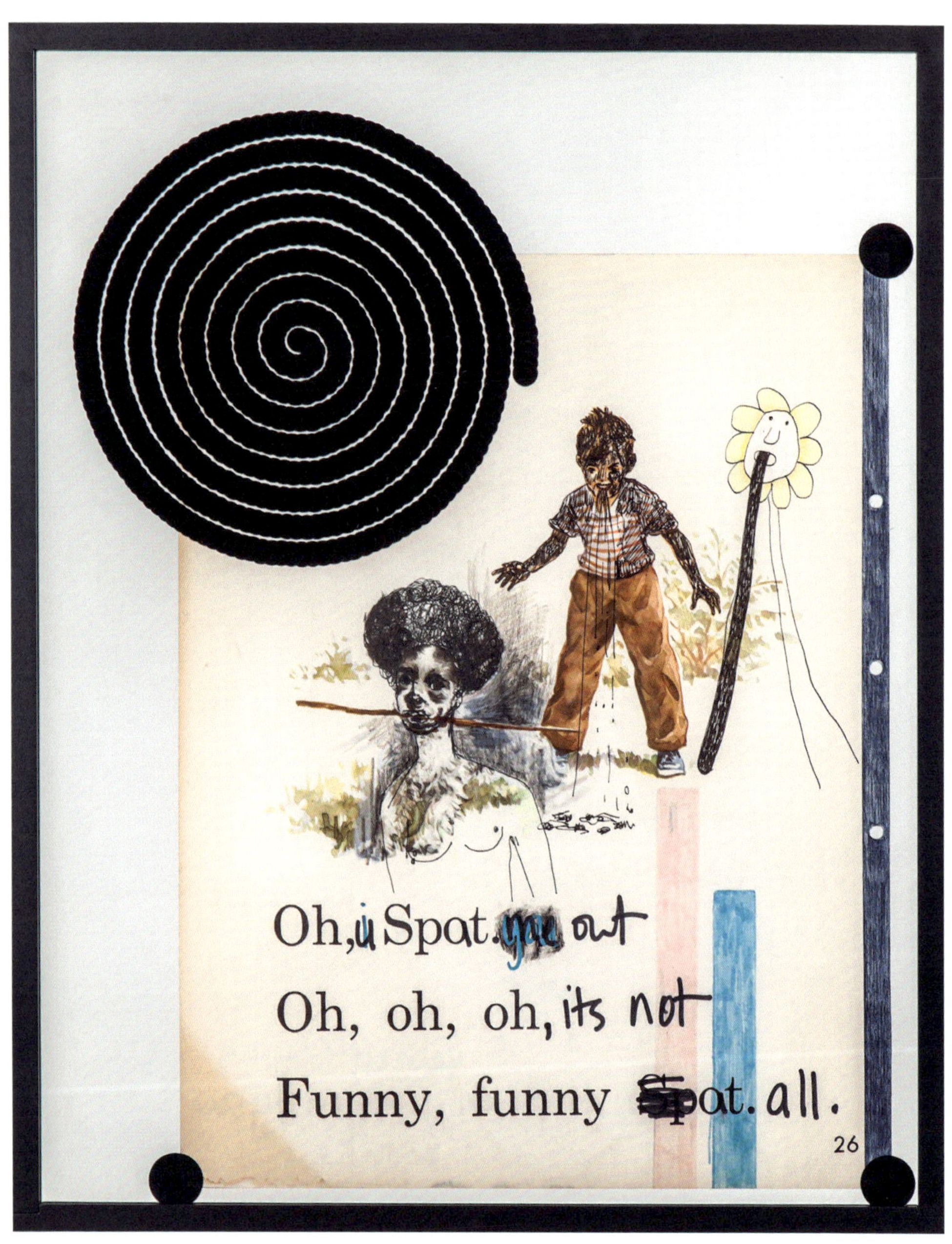

Links in a Chain (4) (detail), 2016
Mixed media
182 × 72.5 × 25 cm

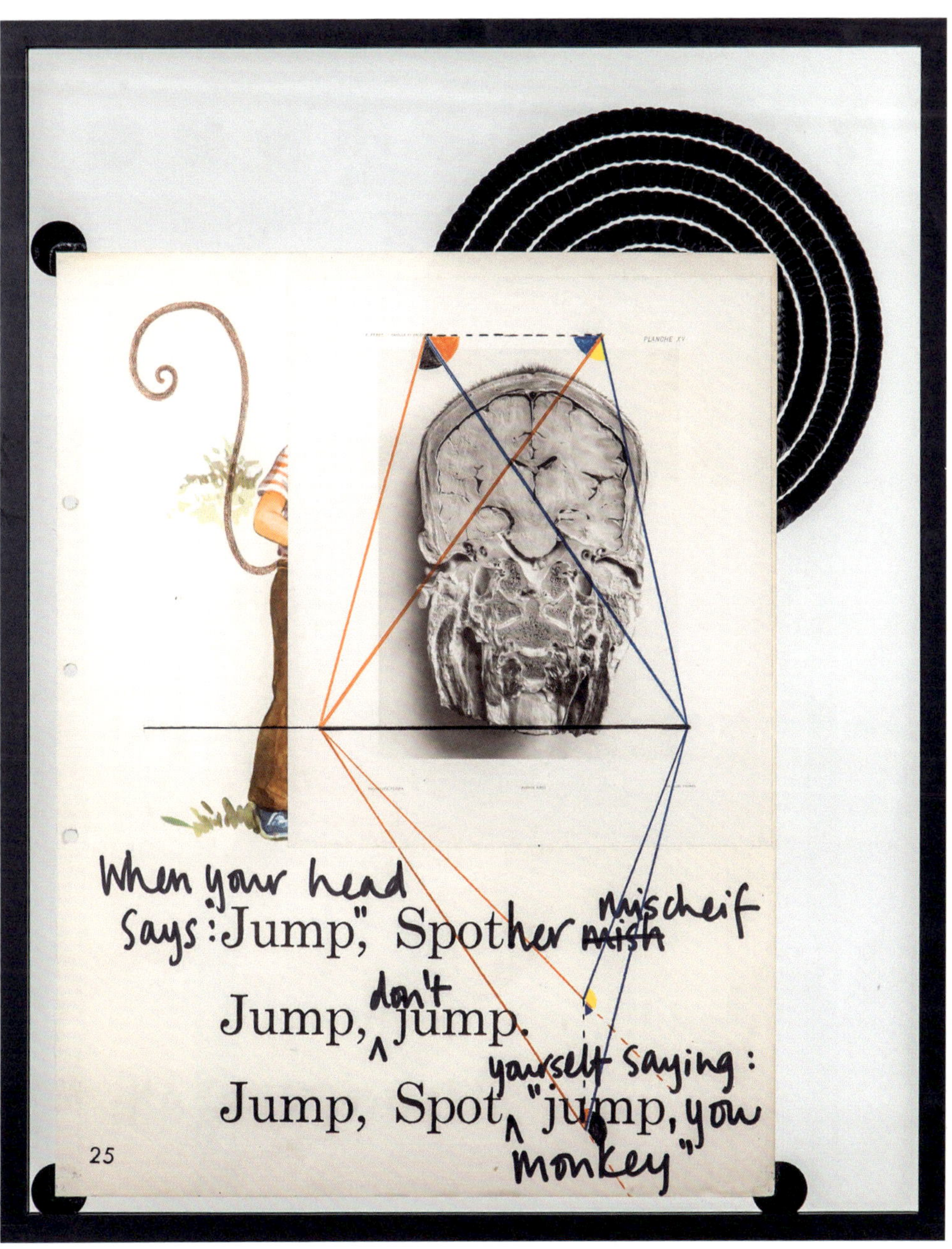

Links in a Chain (4) (detail), 2016
Mixed media
182 × 72.5 × 25 cm

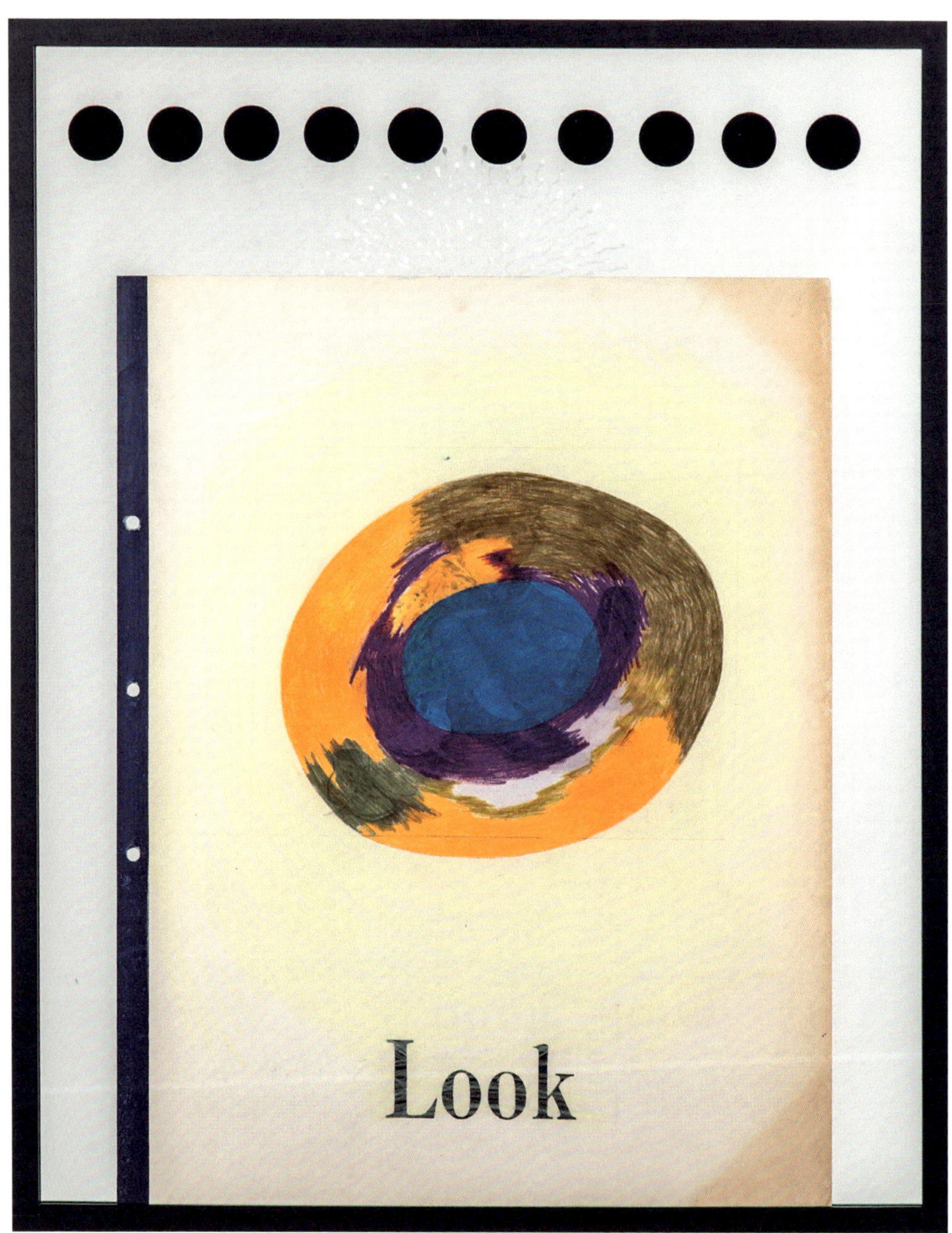

Links in a Chain (5) (detail), 2016
Mixed media
182 × 72.5 × 25 cm

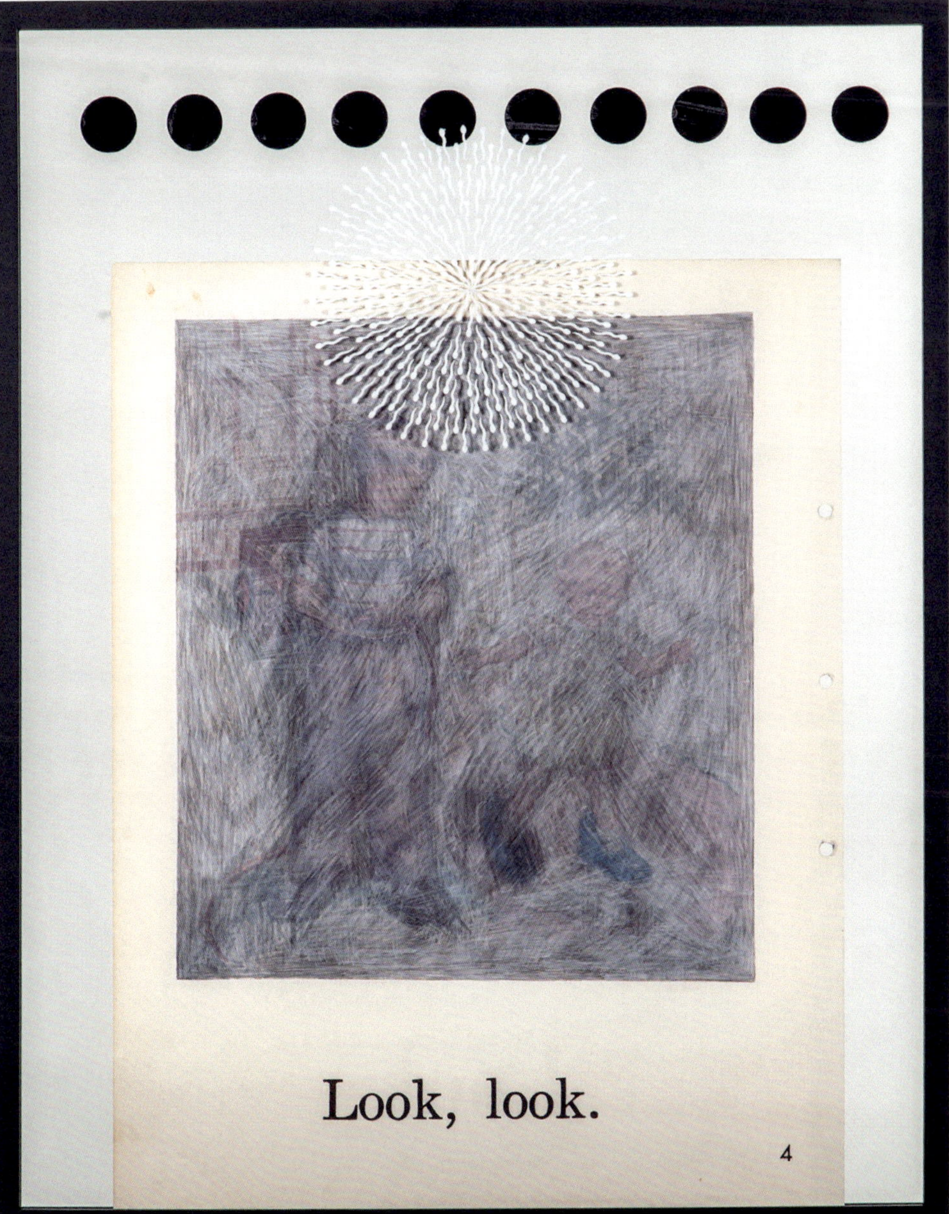

Links in a Chain (5) (detail), 2016
Mixed media
182 × 72.5 × 25 cm

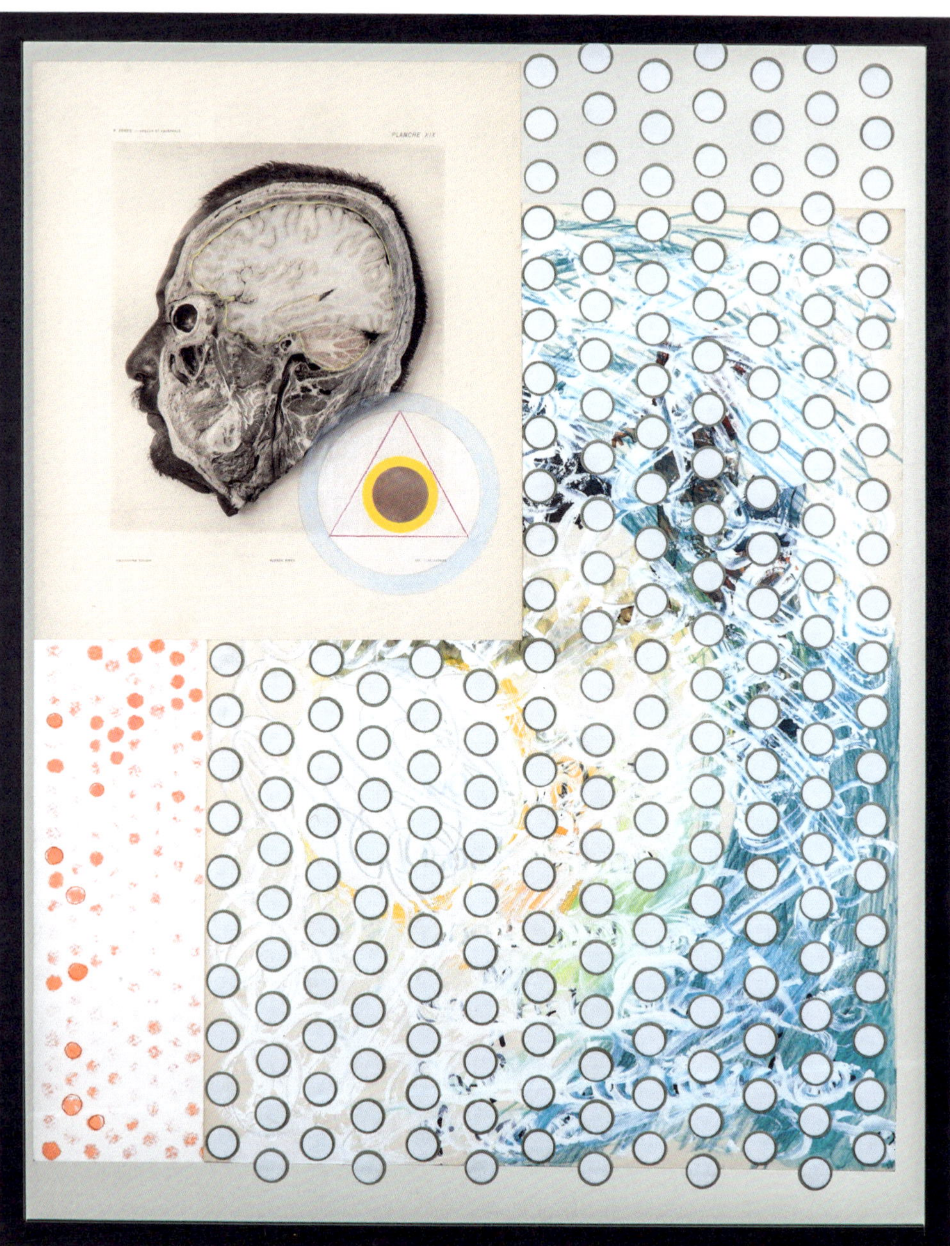

Links in a Chain (6) (detail), 2016
Mixed media
182 × 72.5 × 25 cm

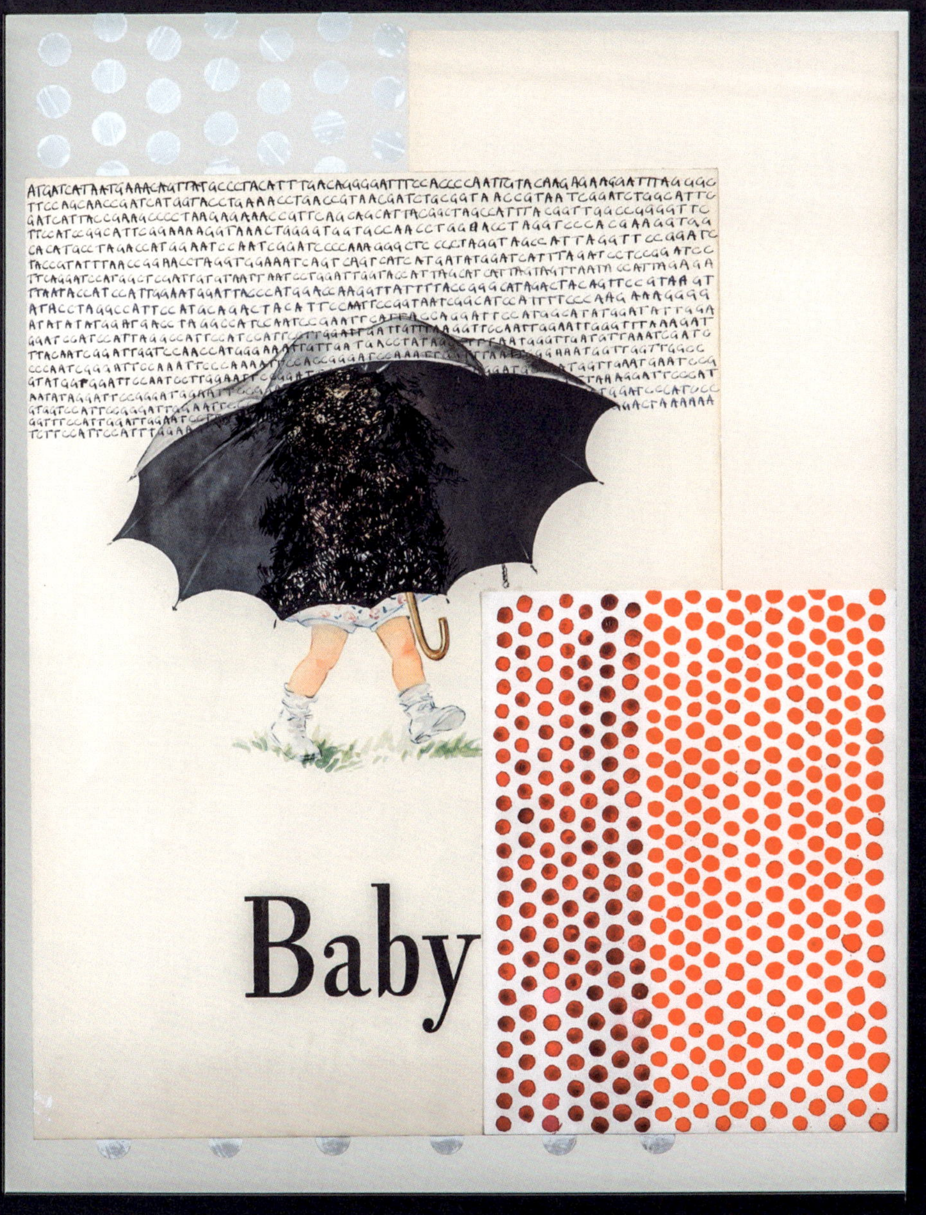

Links in a Chain (6) (detail), 2016
Mixed media
182 × 72.5 × 25 cm

73

15.

Rhizomatic Invasion

Kher pumps blood and life through the building. Her works are not commentaries but run a parallel course to things that already exist. From time to time strange, fascinating, discomforting, wonderful connections arise when Kher posits works that are in complete accord with the "real" world. Her exhibition is a bit like a drawing on acetate, which is placed over an existing reality, producing a variety of new elements.

Her work is maybe like marks on the celluloid top-sheet of a magic slate or "mystic writing-pad" that Sigmund Freud referred to: "If we imagine one hand writing upon the surface of the Mystic Writing-Pad while another periodically raises its covering-sheet from the wax slab, we shall have a concrete representation of the way in which I tried to picture the functioning of the perceptual apparatus of our mind. . . . I showed that the perceptual apparatus of our mind consists of two layers, of an external protective shield against stimuli whose tasks it is to diminish the strength of excitations coming in, and of a surface behind it which receives the stimuli, namely the system Pcpt.-Cs. [Perception-Consciousness]. . . . I do not think it is too farfetched to compare the celluloid and waxed paper cover with the system Pcpt.-Cs. And its protective shield, the wax slab with the unconscious behind them, and the appearance and disappearance of the writing with the flickering-up and passing-away of consciousness in the process of perception."[43]

Kher's works are like the marks on celluloid over waxed paper and the museum site is the waxed sub-layer onto which she is adding traces. They are visible during the show and disappear at the end, the same way that marks on the magic slate disappear when the celluloid is lifted. However, some marks will linger permanently in the minds of those who saw them and, others will be left, unintentionally, on the very fabric of the building.

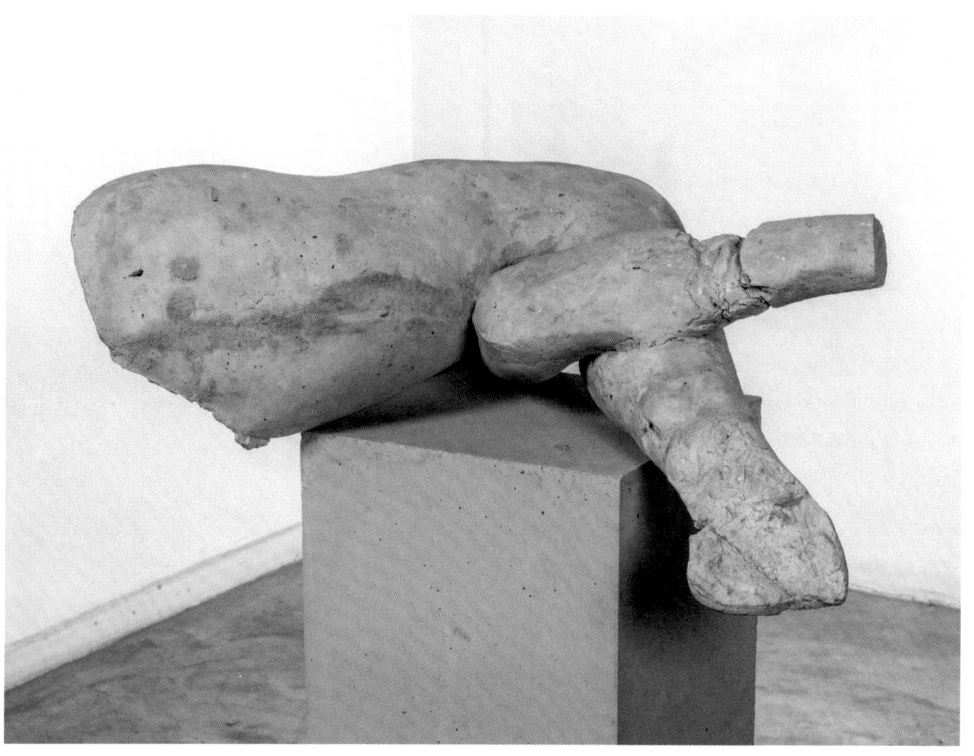

Take something for something, 2016
Concrete
114×66×64 cm

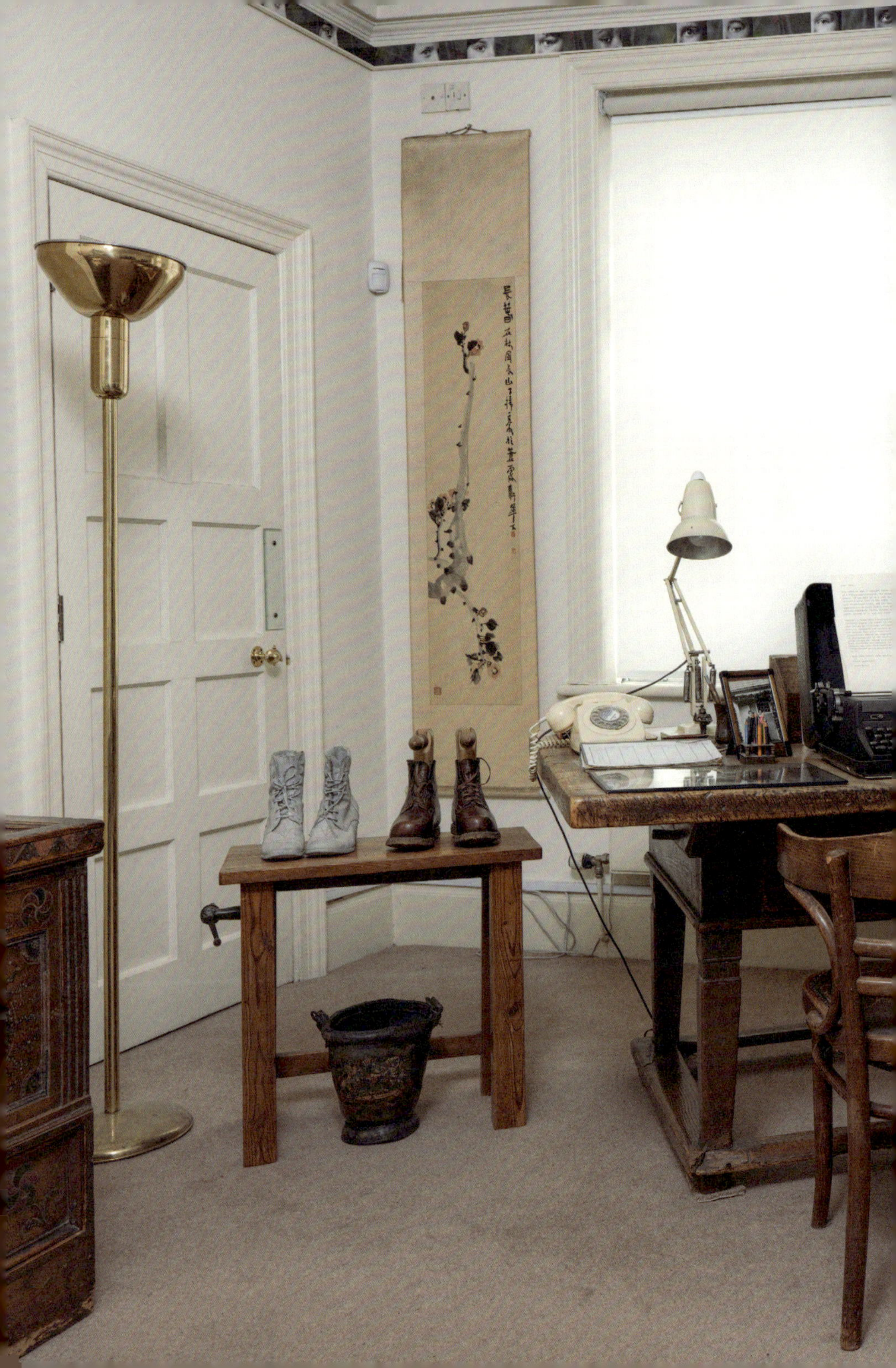

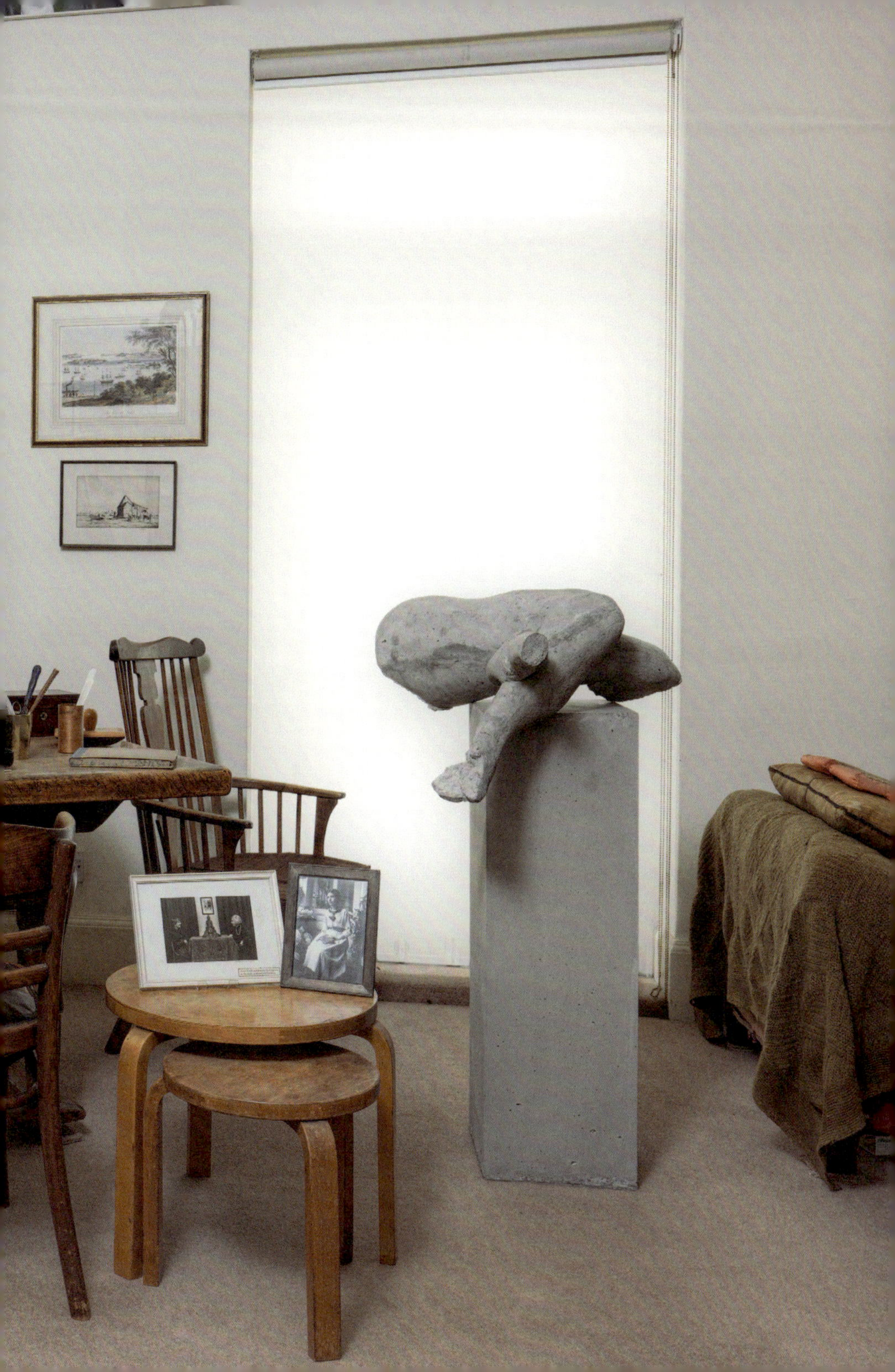

Self-Portrait: Boots, 2013
Concrete
c. $40 \times 10 \times 20$ cm each boot
Display dimensions variable

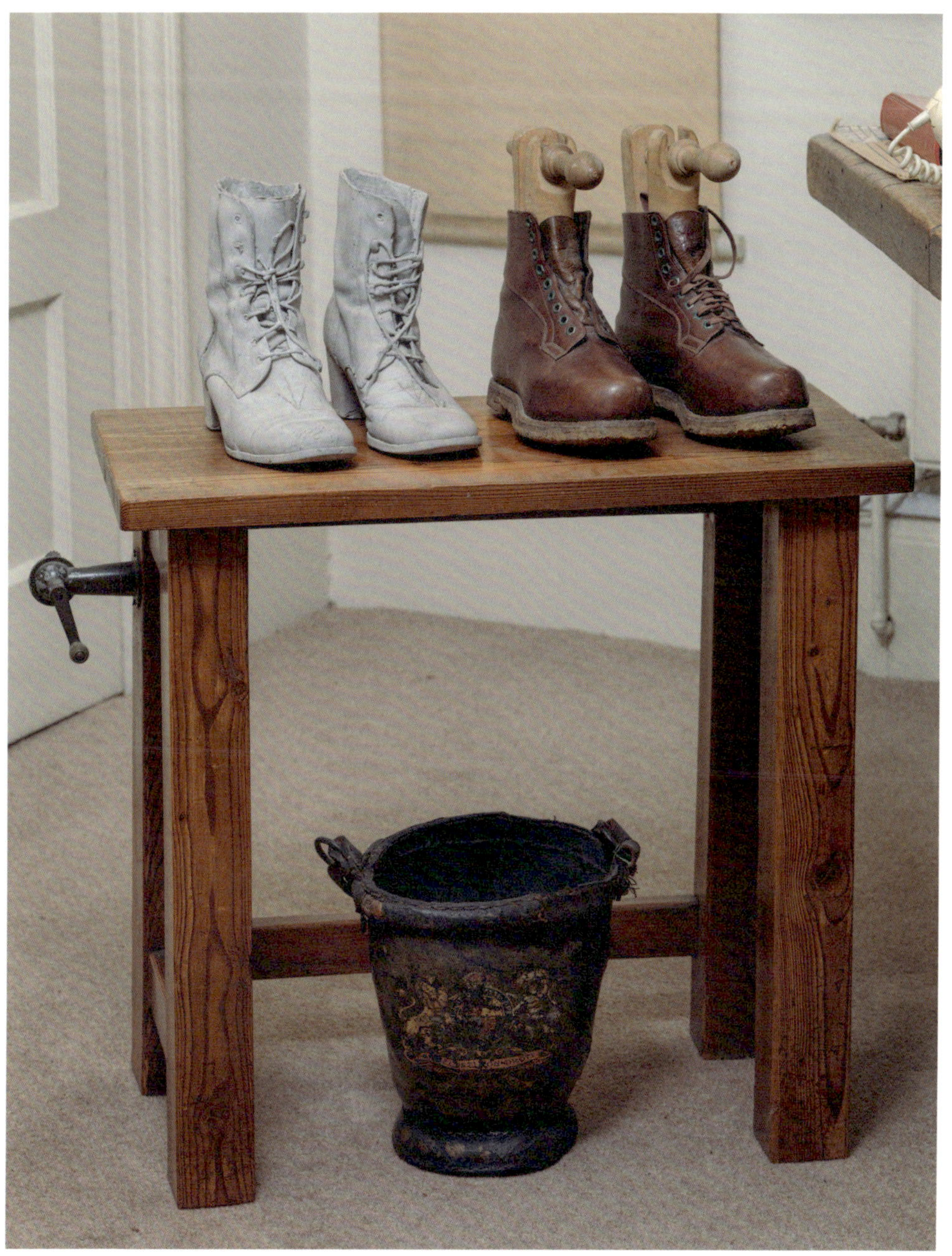

Notes.

1. Maggie Nelson, *The Argonauts*, London: Melville House, 2015, p.4.

2. "I like my own studio and I don't really build my work off-site. There is a part of the work that I have to experience myself, and a certain confrontation with the work that I have to know. My edits of the work happen in the studio . . . Although, of course, there is a moment when you have to move to the exhibition space and let that resonate before taking final decisions . . . Ultimately, it becomes about the intrinsic quality of the object itself and the alchemy that then happens, in the space, with the viewer." (Kher, from interview with Anabelle de Gersigny, on ocula.com, March 2015) [https://ocula.com/magazine/conversations/bharti-kher/].

3. From http://traum-deutung.de/haus/ [translated from German].

4. Gaston Bachelard, *The Poetics of Space*, trans. Maria Jolas, Boston MA: Beacon Press, 1969, p.8.

5. Georges Didi-Huberman, *La ressemblance par contact. Archéologie, anachronisme et modernité de l'empreinte*, Paris: Minuit, 2008, p.27 [All quotes from *La ressemblance par contact* have been translated into English for this essay].

6. Maggie Nelson, *The Argonauts* (see note 1.), pp.16f.

7. Maggie Nelson, ibid., p.16.

8. Kher, sketchbook diary about *Six Women*.

9. Kher, in conversation with the author.

10. Georges Didi-Huberman, *La ressemblance par contact* (see note 5.), p.121.

11. Kher, from interview with Gayatri Sinha, on criticalcollective.in, August 2016. [http://www.criticalcollective.in/NoticeboardInner.aspx?Id=112].

12. Kher, in conversation with the author.

13. Georges Didi-Huberman, "Wax Flesh: Vicious Circles", trans. Brian Holmes, in *Encyclopaedia Anatomica*, Cologne: Benedict Taschen Verlag, 1999, p.65.

14. Kher, in conversation with the author.

15. "I was reading about Descartes' wax analogy. I liked the idea that it was possibly one of the only materials that retains its own property through transformation. It can take the form of two separate properties and yet be the same. No matter whether it is heated or it's cool. And then I am thinking about the green tablet, the emerald tablet or the wax tablets that were used to send code." (Kher, from interview with Gayatri Sinha, see note 11.).

16. Kher, in conversation with the author.

17. http://www.shmoop.com/descartes/quotes.html. *From Meditations on First Philosophy.*

18. https://en.wikipedia.org/wiki/Chimera_(genetics).

19. Maggie Nelson, *Bluets,* Seattle: Wave books, 2009, No. 189, p.76.

20. "First imprint of the skin and then you freeze it and then you cover it so it is almost encased, almost like a time capsule perhaps. Or when you dig up perfectly preserved bones." . . . "You hold it in time. Could nearly be reverse of a cast" (Kher, in conversation with the author).

21. "I have made my own code which means I can write what I like without anyone reading my diaries. So it's like a secret language, it's a language in a lot of pieces that I am making, they are letters to people that I know. They are landscapes." (Kher, from interview with Gayatri Sinha, see note 11.).

22. Georges Didi-Huberman in *Encyclopaedia Anatomica* (see note 12.), p.66.

23. Kher, in conversation with the author.

24. Georges Didi-Huberman, *La Ressemblance par contact* (see note 5.), p.125.

25. Georges Didi-Huberman, ibid., p.13.

26. Kher, diary.

27. Kher, from interview with Susan Silas and Chrysanne Stathacos, on mommybysilasand-stathacos.com, 2013 [http://www.mommybysilasandstathacos.com/2013/11/01/a-conversation-with-bharti-kher/].

28. Byung-Chul Han, first half of quote cited from *The Future is already here – it is just not evenly distributed*, cat. 20th Biennale of Sydney, p.315, Sydney, 2016; second half of quote translated for this essay from *Abwesen*, Berlin: Nerve Verlag, 2007, pp.23ff.

29. Gaston Bachelard, *The Poetics of Space* (see note 3.), pp.7-8.

30. "When I was six and joined school, the only reason I got in, I believe, was because I made a 'beautiful' drawing of a house with a garden and a road. If someone asks me what's the favourite drawing that you drew, it's the house with four windows and the door and a roof with smoke coming out of it. A little path with a gate and fence all the way around, with grass and flowers inside, and the rest of the world is there with you. This drawing of the world is the house with the roof. If there's no smoke coming from a chimney then it comes from a fire somewhere else." (Kher, from interview with Aveek Sen, in *Bharti Kher*, London: Parasol unit for contemporary art, 2012 (exh. cat.)).

31. "I have always known that my body and my experiences are quite small, quite contained. And if I venture very far out of it, I find it disconcerting and actually quite confusing, maybe overwhelming, which is why I like to come to the studio every day, I like to be here a lot of the time. It's my centre." (Kher, interview with Aveek Sen, see note 30.).

32. Gaston Bachelard, *The Poetics of Space* (see note 4.), p.3.

33. "*Bloodline* was made in 2002 for a house in Mumbai that was soon to be knocked down. I made it during a residency in the house and wanted to connect the floor to the ceiling and to mark the space vertically up through a huge staircase. The bangles because they are glass could be lit from inside and that made the work like a blood vessel. I used the work again in the Rockbund to link the single building from the first floor to the 5th. The building as a breathing entity." (Kher, in conversation with the author).

34. Kher, in conversation with the author.

35. Kher, diary, 2014.

36. Kher, diary, 2014.

37. Kher, in email to the author.

38. The Egyptian gilded mummy mask from Freud's own collection is possibly from 600 BC to 332 BC. From her own collection, the artist has placed a bronze breastplate possibly from 19th c., which was used by the performer acting as the Mother Goddess (*Kali*) in a temple ritual dance (*Theyyam*).

39. http://www.philsliteraryworks.com/pdfs/Other/Copy-of1-The-Ego-by-Anna-Freud2-1-other.pdf.

40. Kher, from interview with Gayatri Sinha (see note 11.).

41. Kher, in conversation with the author.

42. Kher, in email to the author.

43. Sigmund Freud, A Note upon the Mystic Writing-Pad (1925), in: *The Archive. Documents of Contemporary Art*, ed. by Charles Merewether, London: The MIT Press, 2009, p.22ff.

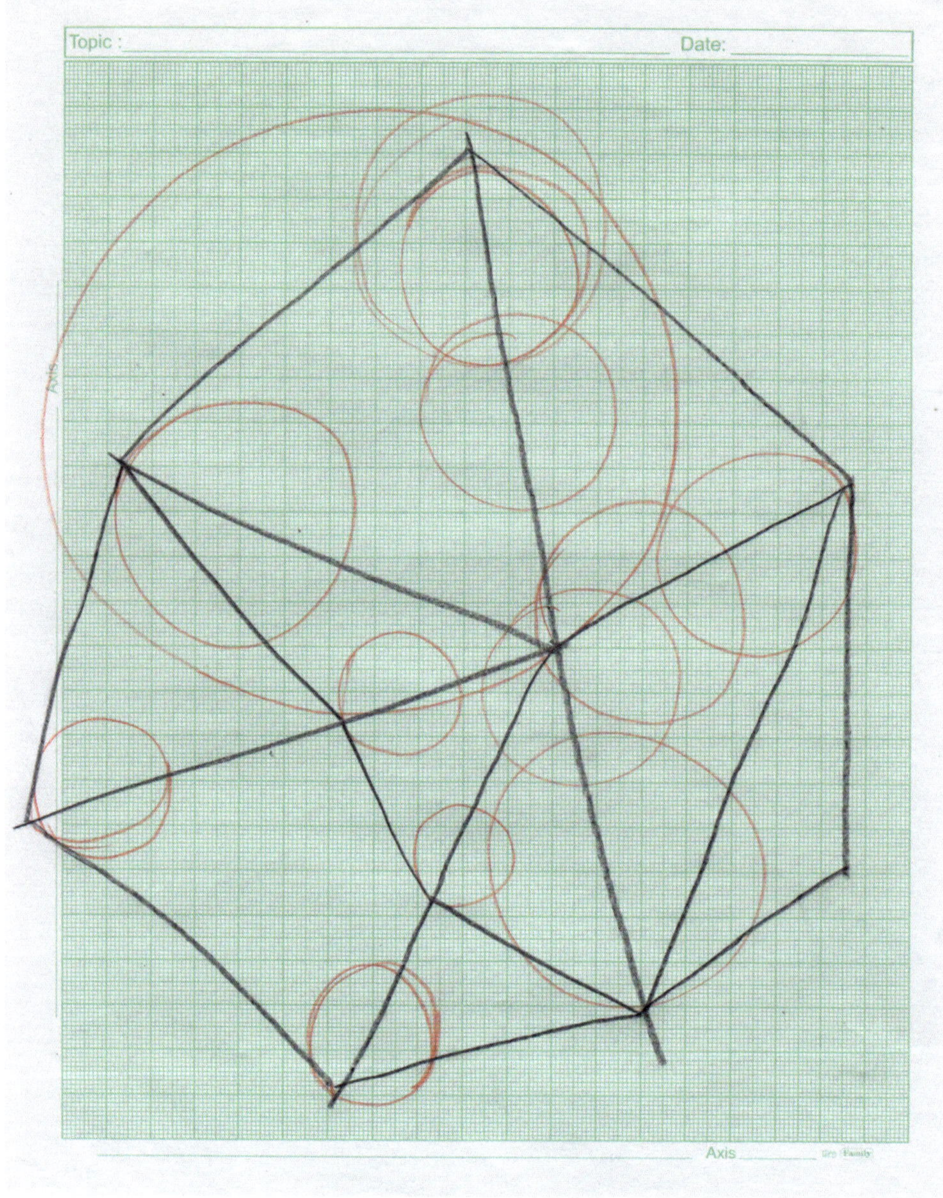

Page from artist sketchbook, 2014
Pencil on graph ruled sheet
26 × 21.4 cm

Bharti Kher. Biography.

Born in London, England, 1969
Lives and works in New Delhi, India, since 1993

Studied at the Middlesex Polytechnic, Cat Hill, London, England 1987-1988
BA Honours, Fine Art, Painting at the Foundation Course in Art & Design
Newcastle Polytechnic, Newcastle, England 1988-1991

Selected Solo Exhibitions

2016	Freud Museum, 'This Breathing House', London, England
	Galerie Perrotin, 'The Laws of Reversed Effort', Paris, France
	Lawrence Wilson Art Gallery, 'In Her Own Language', Perth, Australia
	Vancouver Art Gallery, 'Matter', Vancouver, Canada
2014	Hauser & Wirth, 'three decimal points. Of a minute of a second of a degree', Zurich, Switzerland
	Rockbund Art Museum, 'Misdemeanours', Shanghai, China
2013	Kukje Gallery, 'Anomalies', Seoul, Korea
	Nature Morte, 'Bind the Dream State to your Waking Life', New Delhi, India
2012	Galerie Perrotin, 'Many, (too) many, more than before', Hong Kong, China
	Hauser & Wirth, 'The hot winds that blow from the West', New York NY
	Parasol unit foundation for contemporary art, London, England
	Savannah College for Art and Design, 'Reveal the secrets that you seek', Savannah GA
2011	Galerie Perrotin, 'Leave your smell', Paris, France
2010	Gallery Ske, 'disturbia, utopia, house beautiful', Bangalore, India
	Hauser & Wirth, 'inevitable undeniable necessary', London, England
2008	Baltic Centre for Contemporary Art, 'Virus', Gateshead, England
	Galerie Perrotin, 'Sing to them that will listen', Paris, France
2007	Jack Shainman Gallery, 'An Absence of Assignable Cause', New York NY
	Nature Morte, 'An Absence of Assignable Cause', New Delhi, India
2006	Gallery 88 and Gallery Ske, 'Do not Meddle in the Affairs of Dragons, Because You Are Crunchy and Taste Good with Ketchup', Mumbai, India
2004	Gallery Ske, 'Quasi-, mim-, ne-, near-, semi-, -ish, -like', Bangalore, India
	Nature Morte, 'Hungry Dogs Eat Dirty Pudding', New Delhi, India
2001	Gallery Chemould, 'The Private Softness of Skin', Mumbai, India
2000	Bose Pacia Gallery, 'The Private Softness of Skin', New York NY

2016   20th Biennale of Sydney, 'The Future Is Already Here – It's Just Not Evenly
        Distributed', Sydney, Australia

2015   Villa Reale's Galleria d'Arte Moderna, 'Don't Shoot the Painter – UBS Art
        Collection', Milan, Italy
        Gallery Ske, 'Codes of Culture', New Dehli, India
        Art Gallery of New South Wales, 'Go East – The Gene & Brian Sherman
        Contemporary Asian Art Collection', Sydney, Australia

2014   Kochi Biennale Foundation, 'Kochi-Muziris Biennale', Kochi, India
        Guggenheim Abu Dhabi, 'Seeing through Light', Abu Dhabi, UAE
        The Old Sorting Office, 'Here Today… A Major exhibition marking 50 years of
        the IUCN Red List', London, England

2013   Hauser & Wirth, 'Trade Routes', London, England
        Khoj International Artists' Association, 'We are Ours: A Collection of Manifestos
        for the Instant', New Delhi, India
        Kunstmuseum Wolfsburg, 'Art & Textiles – Fabric as Material and Concept in
        Modern Art from Klimt to the Present', Wolfsburg, Germany
        Museum of Contemporary Canadian Art, 'Misled by Nature: Contemporary Art
        and the Baroque', Toronto, Canada (Travelling Exhibition)

2012   Arken Museum of Modern Art, 'India: Art Now', Arken, Denmark
        Art Gallery of Alberta, 'Misled by Nature: Contemporary Art and the Baroque',
        Edmonton, Canada (Travelling Exhibition)
        Mystetskyi Arsenal, 'First International Biennale of Contemporary Art: The Best
        of Times, The Worst of Times. Rebirth and Apocalypse in Contemporary Art',
        Kiev, Ukraine
        Tel Aviv Museum of Art, 'Massive/Intensive: Contemporary Art from India',
        Tel Aviv, Israel
        Wilhelm-Hack-Museum, 'Dot. Systems. From Pointillism to Pixelation',
        Ludwigshafen, Germany

2011   Centre Pompidou, 'Paris – Delhi – Bombay', Paris, France
        Essl Museum, 'Festival der Tiere', Klosterneuburg, Austria
        The John F. Kennedy Center for the Performing Arts, 'Maximum INDIA',
        Washington DC
        Kemper Museum of Contemporary Art, 'Pattern ID', Kansas City MO
        (Travelling Exhibition)
        Kiran Nadar Museum of Art, 'Time Unfolded', New Delhi, India
        MAXXI Museo Nazionale delle Arti del XXI Secolo, 'Indian Highway V', Rome,
        Italy (Travelling Exhibition)
        Musée d'Art Contemporain, 'Indian Highway IV', Lyon, France
        Nature Morte, 'Seduction by Masquerade', New Delhi, India

| 2010 | Akron Art Museum, 'Pattern ID', Akron OH (Travelling Exhibition) |

2010 Akron Art Museum, 'Pattern ID', Akron OH (Travelling Exhibition)
      Gothenburg City Hall, 'Gothenburg Culture Festival', Gothenburg, Sweden
      Herning Kunstmuseum, 'Indian Highway III', Herning, Denmark
      (Travelling Exhibition)
      Kunstmuseum Luzern, 'Lebenszeichen. Altes Wissen in der zeitgenössischen Kunst /
      Signs of Life. Ancient Knowledge in Contemporary Art', Lucerne, Switzerland
      Kunstmuseum Thun, 'Susan Hefuna – Bharti Kher – Fred Tomaselli: Between the
      Worlds', Thun, Switzerland
      Museum of Contemporary Art, 'Tokyo Art Meeting. Transformation', Tokyo, Japan
      Queensland Art Gallery, Gallery of Modern Art, '21st Century: Art in the first
      Decade', Queensland, Australia
      The Saatchi Gallery, 'The Empire Strikes Back: Indian Art Today', London,
      England
2009 Lalit Kala Academy, 'Marvellous Reality', New Delhi, India
      Astrup Fearnley Museum, 'Indian Highway II', Oslo, Norway (Travelling Exhibition)
      Essl Museum, 'Chalo! India: A New Era of Indian Art', Klosterneuburg, Austria
      (Travelling Exhibition)
      Marianne Boesky Gallery, 'Group Show: Bharti Kher, Yayoi Kusama,
      Eva Rothschild, Mindy Shapero', New York NY
      Museum on the Seam, 'Nature Nation', Jerusalem, Israel
      National Museum of Contemporary Art, 'Chalo! India: A New Era of Indian Art /
      Open Your Third Eye', Seoul, Korea (Travelling Exhibition))
      Palais des Arts de Dinard, 'Who`s Afraid of the Artists? A Selection of Works from
      the Pinault Collection', Dinard, France
      Yale University School of Art, 'Shifting Shapes. Unstable Signs', New Haven CT
2008 Busan Biennale, 'Expenditure', Busan, Korea
      Devi Art Foundation, 'Still moving Image', New Delhi, India
      Devi Art Foundation, 'Where in the World', New Delhi, India
      Haus der Kulturen der Welt, 'Re-imagining Asia. A Thousand Years of Separation',
      Berlin, Germany (Travelling Exhibition)
      Institut Valencia d'Art Modern, 'India Moderna', Valencia, Spain
      Mori Art Museum, 'Chalo! India: A New Era of Indian Art', Tokyo, Japan
      (Travelling Exhibition)
      Serpentine Gallery, 'Indian Highway', London, England (Travelling Exhibition)
2007 Art Gallery of Ontario, 'Hungry God', Toronto, Canada
2006 Arario Gallery, 'Hungry Gods', Beijing, China
      Lille 3000, 'Le Troisième Oeil', Lille, France
      Queensland Art Gallery, 'The 5th Asia-Pacific Triennial of Contemporary Art',
      Brisbane, Australia
2005 L'École des Beaux Arts, 'Indian Summer', Paris, France
      IFA Galerie, 'Zeitsprünge, Raumfolgen', Berlin, Germany
      Nature Morte, 'Summer Show', New Delhi, India

2004   Gallery Chemould, 'Crossing Generations: Diverge', Mumbai, India

2003   Henie Onstad Kunstsenter, 'The Tree from the Seed: Contemporary Art
        from India', Hovikodden, Norway

2002   Habitat Centre, 'Sidewinder', New Delhi, India (Travelling Exhibition)
        Khoj Studios, 'Khoj Residency Show', New Delhi, India
        Nature Morte, 'Photosphere', New Delhi, India
        NGMA Mumbai, 'Cutting Edge Contemporary', New Delhi, India
        Sumukha Gallery, 'Glue', Bangalore, India

2000   Kundan Pan Shop, 'Aar Paar. An Exchange Between five Indian and Pakistani
        Artists', Karachi, Pakistan
        Lakeeren Art Gallery, 'Open Circle Exhibition', Mumbai, India

1998   British Council, 'Edge of The Century', New Delhi, India

1996   Edinburgh College of Art, 'Royal Overseas League Open Exhibition', Edinburgh,
        England

Awards

2015   Chevalier dans l'Ordre des Arts et des Lettres
        (Knight of the Order of Arts and Letters)

2010   ARKEN Art Prize

2007   YFLO Woman Achiever of the Year

2003   The Sanskriti Award

Published on the occasion of the exhibition

Bharti Kher
This Breathing House
30 September – 20 November 2016

Freud Museum London
20 Maresfield Gardens
London NW3 5SX
www.freud.org.uk

Design: Matt Watkins
Print and production: Wonderful Books, Netherlands

All works © Bharti Kher 2016
'A Rhizomatic Invasion' © Stephanie Rosenthal 2016
Translated from the German by Fiona Elliott
Publication © Hauser & Wirth Publishers 2016

Photography: Alex Delfanne: cover, back cover, pp.7, 10-11, 30-31, 41, 45, 47, 49, 51, 52-53, 54, 56, 57, 58-59, 79. Jeetin Jagdish: pp.15, 16, 17, 20, 22, 23, 26, 34, 35, 38, 39, 62, 63, 64, 65, 66, 67, 68, 69, 70, 71, 72, 73, 75, 76-77. Francis Till: p.3.

The artist would like to thank Stephanie Rosenthal; Tom Hunt and Julia Lenz
at Hauser & Wirth; Ribhu Borphukon and the team at Bharti Kher Studio;
The Freud Museum London family and her parents for their leap of faith.

Published by Hauser & Wirth Publishers
Edition of 1500

ISBN: 978-3-9524461-5-7

HAUSER & WIRTH

FREUDMUSEUM
LONDON